THE AMERICAN JUMPING STYLE

Also by George H. Morris:

George Morris Teaches Beginners to Ride

Hunter Seat Equitation

THE AMERICAN JUMPING STYLE

~

CLASSIC TECHNIQUES OF SUCCESSFUL HORSEMANSHIP

~

George H. Morris

including

*Stable Management
and Show Presentation*

by Susan E. Harris

DOUBLEDAY

New York
London
Toronto
Sydney
Auckland

PUBLISHED BY DOUBLEDAY
a division of Bantam Doubleday Dell Publishing Group, Inc.
1540 Broadway, New York, NY 10036

DOUBLEDAY and the portrayal of an anchor with a dolphin are trademarks of Doubleday, a division of Bantam Doubleday Dell Publishing Group, Inc.

All photographs by Bob Langrish except where otherwise noted.

Library of Congress Cataloging-in-Publication Data

Morris, George H.
    The American jumping style : classic techniques of successful horsemanship / George H. Morris ; including stable management and show presentation by Susan E. Harris. — 1st ed.
        p.   cm.
    Includes index.
    1. Horsemanship.   I. Harris, Susan E.   II. Title.
    SF309.M789   1993
    798.2'5—dc20   92-42850   CIP

ISBN: 0-385-41082-4

*This book must be dedicated
to William C. Steinkraus,
the man who epitomized style on horseback,
both on the flat and over fences.*

Preface

I began riding in the late 1940s, so I saw for myself and experienced firsthand the postwar evolution of the American Jumping Style. To be riding, teaching, and showing today, and to see how this style has permeated almost every corner of the globe, is truly amazing. It is sound proof indeed of the fundamentals this system advocates.

Before and just after the Second World War, most American hunter, jumper, and equitation enthusiasts rode some form of the English Hunting Seat. In fact, characteristics of this seat lasted well into the 1950s. Nowadays it is rare to see even its remnants in the hunting field—never, never in the American show ring. Riders with their toes down, their eyes down, and their weight on their buttocks—riders whose horses were bent to the outside and given little freedom over a jump—were all too characteristic. For those who can't remember, it was a picture out of the distant past—the Dark Ages. There had to be something better, and there was.

What the Anglo-Irish hunting and racing scene had given us in North America was the love of galloping. None of us English-speaking peoples were of the classical school manege mentality; we would leave that to the continentals. What we had not yet been given was the best technique for riding a galloping, jumping horse. Early on, the Italians had developed the best way of coping with this form of equitation with the Forward Seat discoveries of Federico Caprilli around the turn of the century. Most of the countries of Europe adopted these ideas, translating them into their own riding technology, each in a slightly different way. France adapted the Forward Seat with the most elegance and grace, and it is from that country that our own cavalry officers learned the most. The style of the French seat and the use of aids practiced by their riders suited us and our horses best, since both the French and we Americans had to deal primarily with hot, sensitive Thoroughbred horses.

I do not want to downplay the influence of the Italian Cavalry School (Tor de Quinto) in the evolution of the American Jumping Style earlier in this century. It was the cornerstone of everything to come in galloping and jumping equitation. Nevertheless, it is just so apparent to me how powerful an influence the French Cavalry School (Saumur) exerted over our Army officers and our own cavalry school (Fort Riley) before and between the World Wars. In the position of the rider, the use of aids, and schooling on the flat, so much of what came to America by the spoken word, the written page, and the example of successful horsemen was definitely French. And in this we were so lucky! The principles of French riding are not only the most effective (especially for hot and sensitive horses), but by far the most beautiful. This was important to us in America. Much of our time was spent in the show ring pleasing the judges' eyes, riding hunter and hunter seat equitation classes.

It was not until late in the 1950s that the German influence began to be felt in this country, through the influence of Bertalan de

Némethy, Richard Watjen, Fritz Stecken, and other colleagues of the Austrian-Hungarian-German alliance. From them we learned discipline, management, work ethic, gymnastics, and again discipline—but not always and not necessarily style, which had come before.

I believe the greatest architect of the American Jumping Style (despite what you may or may not hear from his critics) was a man named Gordon Wright. He was a born teacher—in fact, a genius. First and simply, he was a great horseman. More importantly, he was the greatest communicator I have known, and he could impart knowledge better than anyone else. His background was a blend of Wild West cowboy, self-made hunter/jumper rider, trainer, teacher, and finally, graduate of the U.S. Cavalry School at Fort Riley—where, I presume, he was polished up and formally taught what he had only guessed at before. He came out of the war years with a wonderful, practical recipe for making horsemen and horsewomen who rode what was then called "the modern Forward Seat." Of course, there were other lights advocating this type of riding, especially Captain Vladimir S. Littauer (who taught Bernie Traurig) and Jane Marshall Dillon (who taught Joe Fargis and Kathy Kusner). Nevertheless, Gordon Wright gave more to the masses than any of the others. Not only was he a great show ring rider and winner himself, but his students won more Medals and Maclays than those of any other instructor, and he taught more great teachers than anyone else. A prolific writer he wasn't, but he contributed his fair share, and what he did write was excellent. He was truly an all-American horseman and teacher, and a cornerstone of the American Jumping Style of today.

Coming back from the 1992 Olympic Games in Barcelona, and having taught and ridden in Europe a great deal over the past decade, I realized what a profound influence our American horsemanship has had on the rest of the world. In just a few years, we have given back to riding what other countries had given to us during this entire century, and before.

It is impossible for me to walk through the stable area at any world event and see the veterinarians and farriers at work, watch the riders working on the flat and over jumps, and watch the performances of horses and riders without realizing (and smiling inside about) what a tremendous influence we Americans have had in recent years on the galloping and jumping type of equitation. Be it in Australia, New Zealand, Japan, Mexico, Germany, Belgium, France, or Ireland, I see this influence and I am proud.

Believe me, I do not say this in any boastful way whatsoever. We have simply crystallized, modernized, and refined all the good old ideas and given them back intact—and better. You can, therefore, see how much we appreciate our own riding heritage and the peoples who gave it to us. It is not called anything but sharing, giving, and taking.

Hence this book, in which I am writing about the American Jumping Style. In no way is it intended to be a basic "how to ride" primer. There are lots of those around already. In fact, to clarify any points in this book that they find unfamiliar, readers may want to refer to my book *Hunter Seat Equitation* (also published by Doubleday). The technical terms and "how-tos" are fully explained there, as well as both fundamental and sophisticated concepts and techniques, and there are photos to illustrate them.

Rather, this is a book that explains the whys and wherefores of the American Jumping Style of riding, jumping, and general horsemanship. Hopefully, it is a book from which the layman and the novice rider can enjoy learning something about the basics of the style, while the more expert horseman will be able to study every minute detail of horsemanship that brings this style into being. This book is meant to be a study of a system, not a step-by-step "how-to" book.

Once again, as in my earlier books, I must acknowledge and always respect my teachers. From them I formulated and crystallized my own philosophy and methodology, which in turn I was able to pass on, hopefully in a simple, structured, and organized form.

- Margaret Cabell Self, who first got me going.

- V. Felicia Townsend, my first real riding instructor.

- Otto Heuckeroth, who taught me more about the horse.

- Gordon Wright, the man who made me.

- Victor Hugo-Vidal and Ronnie Mutch, early mentors.

- Bill Steinkraus, my guiding light (and at whose suggestion I wrote this book).

- Bertalan de Némethy, the man who made me an Olympian.

- General Humberto Mariles Cortes, an early idol, and Captain Piero d'Inzeo, another idol. Both of these men "followed" their horses to the jumps—something hard to explain, hard to do, and even harder to teach!

- Gunnar Andersen, the incomparable dressage master, who was my last real teacher.

Since then I have relied on my horses, students, and associate trainers to teach me. And they're doing a good job. Actually, it is the fiercest competitor himself, the one who beats you, who proves to be your most valuable example.

My only hope here, as with other books, articles, and clinics, is to be of help to fellow horsemen. In this business, we are always groping in the dark; maybe the text and photos here will shed some light.

George H. Morris
Pittstown, New Jersey

Contents

PART II:
Stable Management and Show Presentation
by Susan E. Harris

THE AMERICAN JUMPING STYLE

PART I

~

*The American
Jumping Style*

Chapter 1

~

*Evolution
of the American
Jumping Style*

~

God blessed the American people, perhaps too much. Most Americans are brought up to value honesty, hard work, open-mindedness, self-discipline, cleanliness, thoroughness, sympathy, and comfort. Of course, any of these virtues can swing to the extreme and become counterproductive. Relatively speaking, the average American horseman* is hardworking and sober. "Early to bed and early to rise," "The early bird catches the worm," and the like are sayings we are raised with.

Being citizens of a relatively new country, we've had to be open-minded and learn from all. We are not at the center of the universe or even of the world stage, as many mistakenly might think, but rather an outpost of civilization. Perhaps this will change in time, but it will take time. We are a new country, only a few hundred years old, not many

---

* I should point out that "horseman" is the traditional term long used by horse people, and it applies equally to either gender. While the terms "horseman or horsewoman" and "horseperson" have their uses, they are unwieldy in practice. I hope no true "horseman" of either sex will be offended if I use the traditional term here.

hundreds or even thousands. Most of our citizens are descendants of poor immigrants, not always of the nobility, the upper classes, or even the intelligentsia. We've had to learn things often by trial and error, secondhand, or from a limited source. This has been better for us in the long run, as horsemen and as people. We've had to be self-sufficient, open-minded, and relatively smart to keep up with the rest of the world.

Americans adore their independence more than anything else. Let's face it—that is the whole point of this great land. Each individual wants to be free to have his own ideas and to express himself exactly as he wants. To have a "sheep mentality" is foreign to us in North America. That is not to say, "Individuality at all costs." If an idea, a technique, or a system works better, each individual will make it his own. However, in the crucible of an aggressive, competitive, and freethinking society, new and better ideas are more likely to be born. This is really the essence of the American Jumping Style—it was not the creation of one man.

English horsemanship must be recognized as the great bedrock of American horsemanship. (Whenever I mention English horsemanship, this must also include Irish horsemanship, for although there are tremendous political and emotional differences between the two peoples today, their horsemanship is close enough to be one and the same.) Let's face it—our language and much of our culture came from England, and our riding base came from there too.

What is our English riding base? Well, to start with, thank the good Lord, it is love of the horse, the first and most important basis for good horsemanship. Without love of the animal, and consequently the ability to think like the animal, one's equestrian future is limited; without this mentality it is literally impossible to go to the top. Fortunately, most (although not all) Americans inherited this feeling for the horse from the English, Irish, or Anglo-Saxon influence.

What else did we get from the English besides a horse mentality? How to care for the animal. Love means attention, which means looking after the thing we love. We call it stable management. Americans are great caretakers. Their stable management, on average, is second to none. Our horses have it good, and this is thanks to the English tradition of good horsemanship.

We mustn't forget the kind of riding we started with and learned to love. Many young people in America today, ring-bound, lesson-bound, and show-bound, do not know where our riding originated. Again, it was the English "school" of practical cross-country riding. I don't mean competing cross-country, or a formal "school" of riding. I mean *riding* cross-country to get from point A to point B. The posting trot was invented by English postboys (who rode the lead horses on stagecoaches and mail coaches) out of necessity: to relieve the horse's back and to prevent fatigue for both horse and rider. This riding for necessity and transportation evolved into fox hunting, steeplechasing, flat racing, show jumping, and eventing.

The Old English Hunting Seat was the forerunner to our modern American Hunter Seat. Yes, it lacked the style and grace of what we know today, but it got the job done and saved one's neck. I would call the Old English Hunting Seat the grandfather of hunter seat equitation, not the father. There was an important step in between: the Forward Seat.

As practical and functional as the Old English Hunting Seat was, it remained too crude to stand the test of time in the show ring or even in the hunting field. Legs forward, toes down, knees gripped, seat heavy, back round, eyes down, and hands often set or even pulling back just isn't good enough. Don't forget that the typical English-Irish hunting country demanded that a rider sit more behind his horse in order to survive the country and the fences. While American hunters tend to fly fences like post and rails, stone walls, aikens, and coops at a fast gallop over open grassland, the English and Irish are going up and down, in and out, and around and about. They are dealing with massive hedges, drop jumps, huge ditches, and all kinds of banks, and often with heavy ploughland. One dare not be too far forward with his horse very often, but rather safely behind the horse's motion. So, from the English we inherited a lot from which to build, but being the curious perfectionists that Americans are, we weren't satisfied to stand still with only a part of our inheritance. After all, there were many other countries, cultures, and kinds of horsemanship accessible for us to draw from.

Around the turn of the century, an Italian named Federico Caprilli changed the face of riding throughout the world. Every country adopted his methods to one degree or another; perhaps the translations differed a bit here or there with slight variations of nuance. Nonetheless the message was the same: for all practical riding purposes and disciplines (excepting only the Manege School for dressage and haute école), adopt what was called the Forward Seat. By shortening the stirrups, driving the heels down, leaning forward, and following the horse's mouth, riders had an easier time, and horses did, too. Horse and rider both became less fatigued, went faster, jumped higher, stayed in better balance, and were more comfortable. To the worldwide horse community, this must have been akin to inventing the wheel. Dawn had broken—get off the horse's mouth and free his back!

Freedom being such a part of their heart and soul, American horsemen were quick to appreciate this new way of riding. Our jockeys were among the first in the world to use the Forward Seat on race horses. Before the First World War and between the two World Wars, American cavalry officers were sent to the Italian cavalry schools at Tor de Quinto and Pinerolo to learn this new way of riding. Consequently, the Forward Seat was adopted by the U.S. Cavalry School at Fort

Riley, where our greatest officer instructors and Army Olympic teams were trained.

Although a few advanced civilian thinkers picked up the Forward Seat in the twenties and thirties, especially through the instruction of Vladimir Littauer, it wasn't until after World War II that it really bloomed through the teaching of Gordon Wright and some other horsemen who came out of Fort Riley and started teaching the masses. I can personally remember how many people in the mid-1950s were competing successfully in shows, not only in hunter and jumper classes but even in equitation classes and the Medal and Maclay Finals, riding some version of an old-fashioned English Hunting Seat, especially with stirrups home and toes down. It is hard to believe how quickly things have evolved in such a short time since then. (It is also hard to believe how long a time it took for the Forward Seat really to catch on with the horse show community here in America; the old-fashioned English Style of riding took more than half a century to die its natural death!)

The French invented classical riding. Their genius, coupled with the greatest sense of style and beauty in the world, along with access to all kinds of equestrian sport—racing, hunting, dressage, show jumping, eventing—provided the world with a system of riding, an ideology and methodology, that can't be bettered. The French School, be it manege, jumping, or cross-country, solves every problem one can ever come across with a horse and in the simplest way.

Before World War I and between the two World Wars, at the same time that our cavalry officers were sent to study the Italian Forward Seat of Caprilli, they were also sent to France to study the methods of the French Cavalry School at Saumur. There they not only learned the great principles of French riding and dressage, but also were in a position to follow the French interpretation of the Italian Forward Seat. Having read many French books on riding and jumping as well as

American books (the Fort Riley Cavalry Manuals and the writings of Harry Chamberlin, Gordon Wright, and others), I believe that the greatest influence upon the base of American riding has come from the French School of Saumur; this school is certainly the equal of the Italian influence. Not only have I read much of this literature, but Gordon Wright, an instructor trained at Fort Riley who was my greatest mentor, and General John Tupper Cole, another Fort Riley man, theorized and taught all the same material that I've seen at Saumur. If one sees beyond the untrained riders in France today and looks at those with some sort of formal French riding education, the roots of American riding are there.

While there was some Germanic influence in American riding throughout the years (our officers had been sent to the German Cavalry School at Hanover, too), it was a drop in the bucket when compared to the influence of the English, Italians, and French. This was true up until the mid- and late 1950s, when an influx of German, Dutch, Scandinavian, and central European immigrant horsemen came to our shores. The timing was perfect. We in America were ready for their dedicated, disciplined, methodical, and sophisticated approach. The continental use of dressage, cavalletti, and gymnastics really was and continues to be the icing on the cake for us. It has deepened our seats and given us more control of our horses. However, I firmly believe that we were fortunate again in having the English-Italian-French-German mix. Modern English riding that combines with German methods does not, in my opinion, work so well, and the style is definitely not the same.

We should be thankful to three men in particular: Bertalan de Némethy, Richard Watjen, and Gunnar Andersen, the first in show jumping and the second two in Grand Prix dressage. These men, the Germanic literature, and this school of riding emphasize the rider's seat and use of back and weight above all else. Having studied extensively with all three men, I particularly liked their light approach to the German School.

So, as you can see, the American School is a complex conglomeration of histories, peoples, countries, ideas, and horsemen. One must first understand the roots, background, and evolution of American horsemanship even to begin to study or understand, let alone learn to do, what we do. Our riding style has been the envy of the world for the past thirty years, whether people want to admit it or not. Ever since Bertalan de Némethy brought his team of five young men onto the European jumping scene in the midfifties, people have gaped and gawked at our remarkable style. And while de Némethy is one of the principal architects not only of the American Jumping Style but also of the World Style of this century, there have been many other, lesser-known contributors—such as Gabor Foltyni—to this remarkable way of riding and jumping horses.

While I have not purposely ignored our Western cowboy horsemen or our Western Style of horsemanship, I do not believe it has influenced our jumping sports or our jumping seat very much. However, many jumping horsemen in this country, including myself, have learned from our cowboys. They are horsemen with a great history of riding that goes back through the conquistadors to Spain and Portugal. They have a great understanding of horse psychology, and they have an enormous amount of practical experience with all kinds of horses at all levels of training. For a supplement to one's riding background, working with these horsemen is a tremendous learning experience.

Chapter 2

~

The American Horse

~

Knowing the background, history, and culture of America helps one understand the kind of horse we grew up with and prefer. I say "prefer" because now there is a far greater variety of breed and type on the American show scene than there was fifteen years ago. Having English roots and speaking English, we have been—and still are to some extent—an offshoot of the Anglo-Irish horseman. To a great extent, this can never change; it is a question of heredity and mentality.

English horsemanship, and consequently American horsemanship, are primarily out-of-doors, not so much in the indoor ring or the manege. Riding cross-country, racing, galloping, and jumping are what we are all about. One horse alone has stood the test of time and has proved most suitable for this kind of riding—the English Thoroughbred horse. Although transplanted all over the world since the eighteenth century, he is unmistakably an English invention.

The Thoroughbred horse today is a miracle. Who could have predicted that the product of three Arab stallions crossed with English mares would turn out to be such a unique creation? The quality, refinement, and class, along with intelligence, heart, and stamina, all must be credited to the Thoroughbred when looking at other breeds that are only part Thoroughbred. These are the good characteristics that any successful sport horse must possess.

We are a country of wide-open spaces, perhaps more than any other hunting and "chasing" country in the world, especially when you consider the rolling fields of the Northeast and mid-South, the vast flatlands of the Midwest, and the prairies and ranges of the Far West. All parts of this enormous land have been used for fox hunting, coyote hunting, or drag hunts. All of our hunter, jumper, and equitation horse show divisions were born from the hunting field; the same is true in countries all over the world. Racing and steeplechasing have the same roots.

What kind of horse was needed for such sports in this country? Jumping ability, while important, was no more important than the ability to gallop and stay or the courage and "heart" found in the blood horse. The Thoroughbred horse could gallop low to the ground, cover long distances effortlessly, and not become fatigued; he was also comfortable to ride and beautiful to watch. Our hunting scene, and consequently the simulated hunting scene of the horse show ring, did not favor the cold-blooded, short-coupled, higher-moving, half-bred carthorse type. This "heavy" kind of horse, suited to carrying weight in the trappy country of England and Ireland with its banks, ditches, drop fences, and heavy ploughland, did not fare as well in the more open hunting country of North America. It was the Thoroughbred or seven-eighths-bred horse that we needed, one that could gallop and stand off at the post and rails, walls, coops, aikens, and timber fences more typically found in our hunting fields. These were the horses American horsemen grew up with, and they knew such horses were best for their needs. They hunted and raced them, steeplechased them, played polo on them—and took them into the show ring and exhibited, judged, marketed, and promoted them. Like the peoples of all countries deeply rooted in England, we revere the Thoroughbred horse. He has been put on a pedestal by us, and he is there to stay.

When Bertalan de Némethy arrived on our shores in the early 1950s, he said, "You don't need to go abroad to buy horses. You have the best horses in the world. All they need is correct training." He was speaking about our almost unlimited supply of big, rangy, athletic blood horses. And in the following decades, he proved to the world he was right. Why were they the best for Olympic jumping? Really, for the same reasons that Thoroughbreds or near-Thoroughbreds are usually the best for all galloping horse sports. First, the physical size and type are right. These are big (sixteen to seventeen hands), light, athletic, refined animals. Second, the mental capacity is usually good. While blood horses are often hot and nervous, they are at the same time extremely sensitive and intelligent, and, what's more important, bold. A bold, brave horse is a must for any high-level jumping sport. He must willingly take on anything, yet at the same time be sensitive and careful enough that he doesn't want to hurt himself. There is a fine line, often possessed by the Thoroughbred horse, between a clean-jumping winner and a "chicken"! Third, once a Thoroughbred horse has the size and power or scope to jump really big fences, and the mental capacity to be rideable and careful enough not to want to hit the jumps, he is the fastest horse of all against the clock. No other breed of horse on earth can gallop as effortlessly and, consequently, beat him in a timed jump-off or a speed competition. In my experience with horses over the past forty years, a good blood horse can do what other types of horses can do, yet easier and better.

Yes, there are other good breeds too, in North America and the world over: Holsteiners; Swedish, Danish, Dutch, and Belgian warmbloods; Hanoverians; Trakheners; Polish; Russian; Selle Francais; Anglo-Arabs; English and Irish Draft crosses; South American sport horses; Canadian hunters; New Zealand and Australian breeds; American Quarter Horses; Appaloosas; Saddlebreds; and even ponies. While these breeds often add some bone, size, power, and temperament to a show jumper, it is usually the representative of all these breeds that is closest to the Thoroughbred, the horse with the greatest infusion of Thoroughbred blood, that makes the best sport horse.

Whatever the breed, in today's jumping sport a horse must have the same basic qualities: enough size and power (scope) to negotiate the huge spreads; a good enough disposition (temperament) to be controllable, yet animated enough to want to do his job; light, agile, and catlike (heavy-going horses can't make it today); sensitive and careful so as not to hit the fences. No matter what the breed, all of these qualities demand a close infusion of Thoroughbred blood. That is why the breeding programs of the aforementioned breeds over the last ten or fifteen years have been so interested in gaining access to quality Thoroughbred stallions and high-class blood mares. All countries now realize how important this direction is when producing horses for the jumping sports. And that is why I feel that the American Jumping Style of riding has had, and will continue to have, a tremendous influence on the world of show jumping. As other countries refine their sport horse breeds in the direction of the hot, sensitive Thoroughbreds that we've dealt with for so long, their riding in turn must also become more refined.

It is not only true but interesting to note how a country's and a people's riding style has been created over the years by the type and breed of horses they ride. Styles in small detail vary from country to country, even among next-door neighbors, due to the specific breed and type of horse being ridden. It is very interesting to study such nuances.

The "Thoroughbred countries" in show jumping—France, Italy,

North and South America, South Africa, Australia, and New Zealand —tend to ride with the motion; in the old days, they even rode ahead of the motion. That is, they close their hip angle, lean forward, and get up off the horse's back. While this can be a bit of a compromising position, it works better on hot, sensitive Thoroughbred-type horses, whose backs are often extremely sensitive. Riders from the "half-bred countries," such as Germany, Holland, Belgium, Switzerland, England, Ireland, Scandinavia, and Eastern Europe, are more prone to sitting down deep in their saddles, hip angles open and upper bodies fairly erect. This "driving position" works better on colder, heavier, and often less sensitive horses. We would say such riders are riding behind the motion of the horse, which is by no means incorrect and not to be confused with being out of balance behind the horse, or being "left behind."

In the "Thoroughbred countries," the riders' hands and legs tend to be quieter and steadier, to accommodate their more sensitive and reactive horses, while riders of the "half-bred countries" often need to use their aids more strongly, and consequently more visibly.

While I do believe that a country's style in general evolved because of the horse being ridden, the interpretation of fundamental riding principles and beliefs makes a great difference, too. Toes in or toes out; knees gripping or calves gripping; sit up straight or lean forward; hands up or hands down—all have their adherents. Imagine how many diametrically different ideas are taught by teachers and trainers who are all good horsemen!

Fortunately for us, our interpreters—the American cavalry officers who traveled to study European cavalry methods before and between the World Wars—were smart. They learned well, especially in Italy, France, and Germany, and brought back good and sound principles. So, between what these cavalry instructors taught us and what the average American horse demanded, we learned principles and practices that are the foundation of the American Jumping Style and its success. We learned to ride with neither too long nor too short a stirrup, the basic length being the stirrup's tread touching the ankle bone. We learned to place the stirrup on the ball of the foot in order to more easily drive the heel down, and to turn the toes out slightly, consequently flexing the ankles. Our contact with the horse is with the calf of the leg and the inner knee bone, not just with the knee. As a result, this constant, quiet, and very secure lower leg contact is effective yet less disturbing to the horse than a swinging or pivoting leg. We allow the seat to be deep yet, by the forward inclination of the upper body, light in the saddle, and we provide flexibility of the upper body by positioning it differently for different gaits and speeds. We learned to keep our heads up and use our eyes positively. Last but not least, we maintained a line from the rider's elbow to the horse's mouth, thus establishing the most direct and elastic contact possible. We in America have been brought up with these beliefs now for the better part of this century, thanks to the men who interpreted these ideas from the original European sources.

The softness of aids—really, the invisibility of aids—characteristic of the American Jumping Style has been brought about by this dual force of riding methodology and the Thoroughbred-type horse. To say that one must only squeeze the leg and close the hand to achieve results is great in principle. However, it is much easier to apply in practice on a thin-skinned, sensitive, hot horse than on a heavy, cold-blooded beast. To sink the weight softly into a horse's back is not only classically correct but mandatory on a Thoroughbred; it doesn't matter as much on most cold-blooded horses if one sits down in a heavy and brusque manner. It takes less effort to get a Thoroughbred to notice an aid, but it also takes much less to make him uncomfortable and provoke a negative reaction. With blood horses, even the voice is applied differently—ample, yet subtle and discreet. Short, mild spurs and short

The Horse

The whole reason for style and good horsemanship is the horse. Whatever is mentioned in this book should directly or indirectly improve the horse's lot in life and in doing his job. People get confused. They think style benefits the rider. No, it really benefits the horse.

Straightness

This picture is unusual in that it clearly demonstrates perfect straightness, both in the axis from poll to tail and in the horse's tracking. Only the nose is (correctly) tipped to the right, toward the leading leg. Out of respect for myself, my horse, and horsemanship in general, I always insist on being well turned out, perhaps to a fault.

Relaxation

A horse's expression shows all. Notice his eyes, his ears, and his tail. This horse is truly relaxed because he is accepting the rider's aids—hands, legs, and weight. He is going forward in front of the rider's legs, yielding to the hands, relaxed in the jaw, and truly straight. A more engaged, collected frame is not really necessary for the jumping horse.

Counter-canter

The counter-canter (or false gallop, as it is also called) is a favorite exercise of American jumping riders and all other educated riders. It not only collects and balances the canter, but also renders the horse obedient to the rider's aids while working at the gallop.

Bending

The curve of the horse's spine is uniformly bent from head to tail; his tracking is straight; he is looking in the direction of movement; and the weight is evenly distributed on all four legs. These are the fundamentals of bending. The purpose is to supple, to balance, and to make the horse straight.

Galloping—Behind the Motion There are three ways to ride a horse: with the motion, behind the motion, and ahead of the motion. (Two of these are correct—with the motion and behind the motion.) Here the rider is galloping behind the motion, a position used for power. His hip angle is open and his upper body erect, close to vertical; the weight is mostly in the rider's buttocks.

Galloping—With the Motion The rider closes his hip angle, which places his upper body approximately thirty degrees in front of the vertical. His weight is now distributed more over his crotch than his buttocks. This is a lighter, easier, and smoother position for both horse and rider at the gallop. We should ride with the motion about 80 percent of the time, and 20 percent of the time behind the motion.

An American Rider—European Style The Europeans have adopted our style over the last few years, and we, to a certain extent, have adopted theirs. What is evolving now in the nineties is a universal style and a universal approach to riding and training show jumpers. Leslie Burr-Lenehan has lengthened her reins, opened her hip angle, weighted her buttocks, and lightened her heels, putting herself behind the motion of her horse. She is riding a heavy European Warmblood; this type of "cold" horse invites this style of riding.

An American Rider—American Jumping Style Historically, there has been a big difference between North American riding and European riding. Now the two are coming closer together. Here Lisa Tarnapol demonstrates riding the gallop with the motion. Her upper body is inclined forward, which automatically lightens her seat. She has risen slightly out of her saddle in a two-point contact position. This position should only be used for galloping on straight lines, never for turns or approaching a fence. It is smooth and easier on the horse's back, though not very strong.

Shoulder-out

The shoulder-out is the converse to the shoulder-in. The horse's hindquarters are slightly away from the wall; they should be kept perfectly straight. The forehand is displaced toward the wall. There is a uniform bend from head to tail, and the horse moves on three tracks. In this photo Michel Robert maintains the right fore on the outside track, the left fore and right hind on the middle track, and the left hind on the inside track. Like shoulder-in, shoulder-out straightens, collects, and supples the horse.

Haunches-in

Haunches-in (also called head to the wall) is a most powerful exercise in mobilizing the hindquarters. The horse's forehand (head, neck, shoulders, and forelegs) is placed straight along the wall. The hindquarters are brought in. Again, as with the shoulder-in, the horse is bent from head to tail, but this time, in the direction of the movement. In this photo, Robert could be showing more bend around his inside (right) rein and leg. For advanced work, the horse should move on four tracks—in this case, left fore, right fore, left hind, and right hind.

Extended Trot

Between the ordinary and extended gaits are modified gaits. Whether these involve a lengthening of stride, a medium trot, or a true extended trot really doesn't matter. They are all, in principle, the same thing. The horse's stride lengthens, and he gains ground without hurrying. Notice the tremendous power generated in this horse's hindquarters; he is truly going forward into the rider's hand and is completely round from head to tail. The relationship between the rider's position, his use of aids, and his horse is magnificent.

Half-halt

The half-halt is simply a slowdown asked for by the hands and supported by the rider's weight (back and seat). The rider's legs come into play only to maintain the straightness and engagement of the hindquarters. So whereas the half-halt is made by the hands, all the aids come into play in concert. Robert is clearly showing us all of that in this photo. The horse is showing us his resistance to the half-halt: mouth open, head too low, and hindquarters too light and high.

Collection

Robert is in a truly classical position in order to best collect his horse. His shoulders, hips, and heels are in line, maximizing the power of his legs and weight, and there is a perfect line from his elbow to the horse's mouth. The whole horse has been shortened—his base and his topline. His speed has greatly diminished, but his impulsion is scrupulously maintained through active driving aids. The mouth is open a bit too much, but the head and neck are perfectly placed.

Ordinary Gaits

The Americans inherited their riding style, use of aids, and training methods primarily from the French School. Here Robert and his horse are demonstrating total relaxation, impulsion, and straightness at the ordinary canter. The acceptance of the seat, legs, and hands is evident, as is the rider's classical position. This is self-carriage: the horse carries himself and his rider in a beautiful natural balance. Notice how the horse is bent toward the leading leg—classically correct.

Classical Position in the Counter-canter

The French School instigated our American ideology of the riding and training of sport horses and the correct position for the rider. Robert's stirrup is on the ball of his foot; his heels are down and in, with the stirrup leather perpendicular to the ground. His lower leg is in contact with the horse; his base of support is close to the saddle yet remains pliable; his upper body is in correct position and inclined forward. There is a straight line from the horse's mouth to the rider's elbow; the thumbs are inside the vertical, and the wrists straight. He is looking up and ahead. Again, note how the horse is bent toward the leading leg.

Galloping Position— German Style

Riding at a gallop, Franke Slootaak shows us a beautiful example of the German School. Due to more grip in the knees, the weight is not allowed down into the heels as much as we and the French like. His upper back is just a little round, probably because he is a tall rider. Nonetheless, horse and rider are magnificent. There is tremendous impulsion and engagement, starting in the hindquarters. The horse's back is "up," not "down"; he is yielding his jaw and is bent at the poll. This is a truly round horse.

Two-Point Contact

This is what we call "two-point contact." The rider's two legs are in contact with the horse; his third point, the seat, is slightly out of the saddle. Every good rider and school of riding knows how to ride this way when galloping on straight lines. This is a better example of posture—the rider's head, neck, and back are all in alignment. Again, the horse is very round. This is also a good example of engagement of the hind leg. Slootaak is a masterful rider and a stylist in his own right.

Bending at a Canter

Hugo Simon has provided us with a perfect photo of bending. Starting with the rider: his eyes are up and looking in the direction of movement; his back is straight; the weight is predominantly on the inside seat bone; his hands are in line with the horse's mouth; the inside heel is depressed; and the outside leg is back a bit. The horse is uniformly bent from head to tail and is tracking straight. A giveaway to the European Style is the horse's "bug-bonnet"; Americans don't use them nearly so much.

The Full Seat— Three-Point Contact

The full seat, or three-point contact, is used most of the time— almost always at the walk, trot, and canter. All three points (the rider's two legs and his seat) are in contact with the horse. Simon is deep in his saddle and very erect, a position reminiscent of that used for dressage. This man is one of the few truly great riders on the flat in the show jumping world today, and a great example of the classical German School. Notice how collected and round the horse is.

Modern Italian Style

Georgio Nuti is cantering with the motion of his horse as he should, not ahead of the motion. I emphasize the word "modern" when I mention the Italian School today. Riding with the upper body too far forward, standing up in the stirrups excessively, and being ahead of the motion—all of which were associated with the early Italian School—don't work well for today's show jumping courses. Nuti rides with and even behind his horses in the softest, smoothest way possible. The textbook form shown here at a canter would do any stylist proud.

Behind the Motion

Nuti's leg has come forward, which in turn has dropped the rider's seat and upper body too far back. Posting behind the motion is a good exercise and technique if done correctly. It is a stronger position, but a lot harder on horse and rider if done for long periods of time. I wanted to show this picture for a reason, as it clearly demonstrates the technique; however, it violates many of the principles I hold dear, such as balance, softness, and noninterference with the horse.

Bending

Another perfect picture of bending on a turn. Horse and rider are both looking in the direction of the turn. The horse is bent evenly from head to tail; his jaw is relaxed; his poll is bent; and his hindquarters follow his shoulders. Consequently, he is active, supple, and balanced. However, Nuti's fingers are too open on the reins. While his hands are soft, he is in danger of losing a true contact with the horse's mouth. The fingers should always be closed lightly around the reins.

The Indirect Rein

Nuti gives an excellent example of bending a horse by using the indirect rein. As you can see, this rein operates from one side of the horse's mouth through the withers toward the rider's opposite hip. It not only bends the head and neck to the right but, more importantly, displaces the horse's weight from the right shoulder to the left shoulder. The indirect rein in front of the withers is used for riding around corners and for canter departs.

Bending with the Indirect Rein
The Australian rider Jeff McVean (his hat is a giveaway!) demonstrates very clearly the use of the indirect rein and its effect on the horse. The horse's head and neck are bent to the left; the weight is displaced from the left (inside) shoulder to the right (outside) shoulder, and the horse's hindquarters are active and in line with the shoulders. The four parts of the rider's body—legs, base of support, upper body, hands and arms—are all perfectly positioned.

Overbent
With horses that tend not to flex easily and are apt to be "stargazers," working them in an overbent frame is not all bad, as long as an expert like Nick Skelton is doing the job. Here the horse is straight, active, and engaged behind. The risk of these tight draw reins in average hands, of course, is losing control of the back end of the horse, either to the rear, the side, or both. Unfortunately, North Americans (and the rest of the world!) are adopting draw reins more and more from the Europeans. In my opinion, draw reins are an overrated tool; I don't need or use them.

The Indirect Rein and Lateral Flexion
The interesting thing here is not Pierre Durand's use of draw reins between the horse's front legs, which is fairly common, but rather the ancient French technique of raising the hand when using the indirect rein. This, of course, is why the horse flexes his jaw and lowers his head to the left. The draw reins are immaterial when the horse is schooled to the hands, as he should be! Dropping one's stirrups periodically not only develops security in the saddle, but promotes feel in the rider's seat.

Two-tracking (Half Pass)

Two-tracking (or half pass), as the German Otto Becker is doing here, is the ultimate lateral exercise. Not only must the horse yield his hindquarters sideways from the leg, but he must remain forward, bent in the direction of the movement, and parallel to the wall. This is a beautiful picture of two-tracking to the right. Both horse and rider are in an exemplary position.

Lengthening of Stride

This horse is perfectly straight, both in the axis of his spine and in his tracking. He is also very active behind, and round and supple in front. These ingredients make it so easy to lengthen the stride or to extend the trot (really the same thing). All this rider need do is relax his hands, and his horse will readily extend himself.

Free Longeing   The Swiss rider Markus Fuchs has learned what we've known for years in America with our hot Thoroughbred hunters: putting a free horse, without tack, on a long longe line is often the best way to relax him. This method of free longeing allows horses to buck and play on their own and get rid of any extra freshness. Usually the horse will come out later that same day a different, quieter, and more trainable animal.

Cavalletti

Cavalletti work originated in Italy many years ago. Here the Italian rider Nuti is showing us how important the cavalletti still is. He is working over a single rail on the ground, which is the most basic way. He is working at a slow pace and insisting on a lateral flexion to the left, making the horse yield his jaw over the obstacle. This will teach his horse to turn in the air. Consequently the horse is very, very round.

Head on Head

The single cavalletti (or just call it a "rail on the ground") is so favored as a stabilizing and concentration exercise that horsemen from all over the world use it just before entering the ring for competition. Here the Swiss Willi Melliger and the Italian Nuti relax their horses at the walk while getting them "sharp." Notice the excellence of position in both riders. The American Jumping Style has touched down all over the world.

Cavalletti—Cantering

This picture shows the bridge between cantering or galloping on the flat and jumping a fence. This is the smallest fence imaginable—a pile of poles, or a cavalletti. All the same techniques are being used here by Simon as if it were a real fence—pace, line, distance, balance, and impulsion. The horse's jump is simply another, larger galloping stride, nothing more.

Cavalletti—Turning in the Air

Becker is using this cavalletti to relax his horse's canter, stabilize the approach, and turn in the air. So much can be accomplished using cavalletti without taking much out of the horse. The rider's leg position is excellent here; however, it is not characteristic of the modern German School. His heels are down, his toes are out, and the calf of the leg is in contact with the horse. The grip is (correctly) not all in the knees.

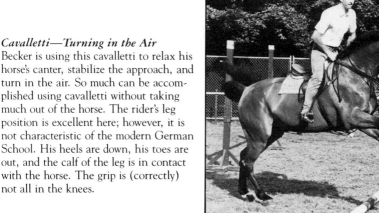

Cavalletti—Angling

There is nothing one cannot do with simple rails on the ground that doesn't simulate actual jumping. A good example is angling. The Belgian Jean-Claude Vangeenberghe really displays an American Jumping Style here in his position, and in his horse's frame, balance, and carriage. Without the excessive use of draw reins, the horse is galloping "uphill"; his poll is the highest point. Also, the rider's weight is predominantly in his heels, not his seat—very French, very American.

Cavalletti—Rider's Position

Vangeenberghe is demonstrating a beautiful galloping position in two-point contact. His seat is slightly out of the saddle, and his two points of contact are his two legs. His stirrup is on the ball of his foot; the heels are down and in, the toes out, and the ankles flexed; the lower leg is in light contact with the horse. His seat is light; his upper body is inclined forward approximately thirty degrees; his eyes are up; and his hands are operating just over and slightly in front of the horse's withers.

Cavalletti—Three-Point Contact

Olympic gold medalist Durand is working in three-point contact at a collected canter on a circle over this cavalletti. His position is exemplary and his horse totally relaxed. The horse must change nothing—not speed, balance, or self-carriage—when the rider shifts from the full seat (or three-point contact) to the half seat (two-point contact). One good test of a horse's training is when the rider goes from one seat to the other without the horse changing. The old French School is responsible for so many good things we see today in show jumping.

The Cross Rail

The basic cross rail is absolutely fundamental to the American Jumping Style. Now the world appreciates its value, which is twofold. First, a cross rail is low, requiring little physical or mental stress for either horse or rider. One can therefore jump many more cross rails than higher fences. Secondly, the lowest point of the cross rail is in the center, encouraging horse and rider to jump on a straight line. Here the Irish rider Gerry Mullins demonstrates near classic form. His legs, base of support, upper body, and hands and arms are exemplary.

Soft Aids

Philippe Rozier of France is a soft rider and a beautiful stylist. Again we can see the proximity of the two styles—French and American. What is especially appealing here over this low warm-up oxer is the softness of the rider's hands and legs. Without soft, sympathetic legs, soft hands are impossible. Aggressive, strong, overdriving legs and spurs are what often produce rough, bad hands. I like the almost slack rein very much; it is a sign of the oft-forgotten self-carriage.

Round

Evelyn Blaton of Belgium is allowing her horse to jump round. Possessed of an excellent lower leg position and a light hand (though I do not advocate open fingers), she is able to maintain the jumping factors beautifully— pace, line, distance, balance, and impulsion. My only criticism of this photo (besides the open fingers) is that her eyes—and, consequently, her head—are down. Interestingly enough, she also takes this position on foot, being a shy woman; this posture fault could be corrected. However, the horse's posture, his bascule, is flawless—something we are all looking for.

The Long Release

We in America have labeled this hand position the "long release." Fuchs of Switzerland rests and presses his hands halfway up the crest of the horse's neck. This technique, which is indispensable for beginners, is also useful for advanced riders in giving maximum freedom to the horse. Note the loop in the reins. This technique has now been exaggerated and caricatured all over the world. Unfortunately, the rider's seat is too far out of and ahead of the saddle (marring an otherwise good photo) in what is called "jumping ahead."

Jumping Ahead

There are lots of things I like about this picture from an instructional point of view: the hands are using the long release; the legs and heels are down; and the rider's back is flat. Nonetheless, a serious fault can be seen clearly from this photo's three-quarter angle: Fuchs is jumping ahead of his horse. His base of support (seat and thighs) is too far out and even slightly ahead of the saddle. Again we see how an excess of motion undermines style, a fault more often observed in Europe than in North America.

A Turning Gymnastic (1)

Fuchs has set up a small vertical followed by a cavalletti on a turn; this exercise could of course be jumped in either direction. The striding appears to be optional: to the outside of the turn in two or even three strides; or to the inside of the turn in one stride. The rider is in a good position with his heels down, his outside leg behind his inside leg, and his upper body inclined forward. The horse is also in a good position, beautifully bent around the rider's inside leg.

A Turning Gymnastic (2)

Fuchs, trained in the American Jumping Style by me, is demonstrating a classic galloping position during this exercise. His legs are back and his heels are down; his lower leg is in contact with the horse; his weight is in his crotch more than his buttocks; his upper body is inclined forward with a flat back; his eyes are up and ahead; and there is a straight line from his elbow to the horse's mouth.

whips are the norm for North America, not ones that are long, sharp, and severe. So one can now better understand the North American obsession with "Be soft, be soft, be soft!" It is instilled in our riders from the beginning as a means of dealing with hot, sensitive, and reactive horses.

North American training methods follow suit. Coping with the Thoroughbred temperament means dealing with hot, fresh, and nervous horses on a day-to-day basis. How does one begin? Usually by turning the horse out in a paddock for an hour or so before getting down to business. This training method "takes the edge off" a hot horse and allows him to relax, work, and concentrate. Longeing is another popular method of choice that allows the horse to "get the bucks out" before one asks him to listen to the rider. Both of these approaches are an indispensable part of the American hunter scene and, consequently, follow over into the jumper world.

The way we ask this type of horse to come together and go to the bit is definitely more progressive, careful, and refined than the approach of the average European, who "puts the horse together" by quicker and stronger means, often using draw reins, chambons, and other auxiliary reins that have only recently (and regrettably) become a part of American equipment. With most Thoroughbreds, force simply doesn't work; equestrian tact does. The English call such sensitive horses "high couraged," a characteristic that can be a double-edged sword. No horse will give you more if you can channel his energy in the right direction, but no horse can fight you harder if you abuse him. Pushing and pulling will backfire and is akin to stepping on the gas and the brakes at the same time in an automobile. Finesse, compromise, and an indirect approach to a problem—"going in through the back door"—will usually get the job done much better than confrontations, force, and fights.

The progressive use of cavalletti poles on the ground and classical gymnastic exercises can make an Olympic star out of a "nut case" when dealing with Thoroughbred "freaks"—horses of extraordinary talent but extremely difficult temperament. (It's been done before!) These horses could not stand nor survive a crash course in learning to jump over big, big fences. Only through the most careful preparation and accurate riding do most Thoroughbreds make it to the big time. Patience, patience, patience is the recipe, not giving the horse a crack with a rail out behind the barn. So whether it is handling in the stall, turnout, longeing, flat work, gymnastics, or showing, the Thoroughbred demands very delicate, precise, and thoughtful management. Not every horseman in the world can deal with this particular horse, and some people should not try. They simply haven't the feeling and mentality for it. I'm certainly not saying that there are not sensitive horsemen in every country of the world who have the capacity to train these horses. It is just that some cultures have grown up with blood horses, so they have had more exposure to this type of horse and understand it better than others. Let's face it: there are Thoroughbred people and non-Thoroughbred people.

The characteristics of the American Jumping Style—position and use of aids of the rider; training methods both on and off the horse, on the flat, and over fences; and especially, equestrian tact—were brought about not only by the riding and training ideology but also by the type of horse. Through the text and photos of this book, these subjects are broken down into specific details in order to be easy to follow and understand.

Chapter 3

~

Components of the
American Jumping
Style: The Influence
of Hunter Classes
and Hunter Seat
Equitation

~

In order to appreciate and understand the American Jumping Style, one really must watch, study, and learn from our hunter division and its derivative, the hunter seat equitation division. These divisions are most instructive whether one is riding, training, teaching, judging, or just spectating. Most North American riders agree that our continued riding of the show hunter is good for our jumper riding. Jim Elder, the many-time Canadian Olympian and medalist, always remarked that he liked to show a few hunters because it helped his Olympic riding career. So did U.S. Olympic medalist Bill Steinkraus. Nowadays, all of our Olympic and World Championship Team riders excel in the riding of hunters. Most of them also won the ASPCA Maclay or the AHSA Medal Hunter Seat Equitation Finals.

Form enables function and function instigates form; they work together. We've also said that a type of people and a type of horse produce a certain approach and a certain style of riding. Our historical background, our type of horse, the nature of our hunt country, and our approach to fox hunting provided the platform from which the show hunter and hunter seat equitation divisions sprung. It is from this perspective that I must paint the detailed picture for the reader to see what our riding style is all about.

According to our national rules, a hunter must be judged, as closely as possible, as a mount agreeable to ride to hounds. He must be mannerly, jump in good form, move low to the ground, and go at an even hunting pace. Any unruliness, unsafe jumping form, poor movement, or unevenness of pace is strictly penalized. The horses are judged over "fly" fences, two thirds of which are verticals and the rest narrow spreads, much like those they would hunt over. Fences are intended to simulate those actually found out hunting, and they usually have a natural appearance; they include post and rails, brush, walls, coops, gates, aikens, and similar fences. Ditches and banks are not frequently found in our typical hunting terrain; such obstacles are now virtually extinct for hunters in the show ring.

In the old days—when time permitted, the courses were long with single fences far apart, and outside courses were the rule—pace was the big factor. You couldn't get close to a ribbon unless you were flying. Now that course designers have shortened the courses and brought the fences closer together with related distances, it's not so much pace but an accurate distance to each fence that wins the blue ribbon. It's now better to be a bit slow and find eight perfect "spots" that match than to carry the pace of old and meet a fence a touch long or a touch short. Precision is the name of the game.

In the hunter seat equitation division, where riders are being judged, the pattern is much the same. Much of the rest of the world sees the major factors in jumping as pace, line, distance, balance, and impulsion. Our priorities in American riding would be line, distance, balance, pace, and impulsion. With distance and balance brought forward, the result of this subtle change of priorities has been beautiful, soft, smooth riding. The strong, aggressive attack approach is definitely discouraged and is nearly eliminated from this particular side of the show scene.

In order to produce what is required for this picture (and don't forget, by the way, the hot, sensitive Thoroughbred-type horse that is part of the picture), the horseman must stick closely to the purest and most classical riding techniques that have stood up under the test of time for generations. Any slight deviation from the accepted principles of the American School of riding promises to backfire. By deviation I mean something as minuscule as the position of the rider's spur, the length of his whip, or how he places his foot in the stirrup. It doesn't succeed, and the rider eventually must come back to the basics.

Because our hunter and equitation rides are judged subjectively, it does not pay to have pieces of tack or equipment that are too obvious, severe, or unusual. Anything too extreme or bizarre is against the rules; moreover, severe or unusual equipment suggests that the horse is unruly or at least difficult to ride. Most horses in these divisions go in snaffle bits (rubber or regular, twisted, corkscrew or twisted wire) or pelhams (rubber, steel, or jointed) with relatively short shanks. Any kind of dropped or figure-eight noseband is forbidden in hunter classes; such nosebands are allowed in equitation classes. Standing or running martingales are permitted in over-fences classes but not in classes held on the flat. Standing martingales are common, as they can prevent a minor head resistance from becoming too obvious to the judge and spoiling an otherwise smooth round; extremely short standing martingales are frowned upon as being too restrictive. Rarely does one see a running martingale in a hunter class as a matter of tradition; running martingales probably went out of fashion years ago because they don't completely cover up a multitude of sins. German martingales are not allowed.

So, although Americans can be imaginative, creative, and daring when it comes to bitting, our upbringing and the reality of competition tend to bring us back to basics and to the simple. Although you do see our jumpers go in anything and everything, that is usually a last, not a first, resort. On our hunters, our tack must be simple, conservative, and attractive, and that habit carries over into our dress code for the jumpers.

What about saddles? Why did we shift away from the basket-type continental saddles so popular in the fifties to the lighter, flatter "close contact" saddle? There were several reasons. First of all, Bill Steinkraus, our first individual gold medalist in show jumping and a great influence on American riders, likes the French Hermes saddle. He claimed that it put his leg closer to his horse, and therefore he could feel the horse better and ride better. He was right! Second, as people were learning and adopting an educated leg, they also found a flatter saddle more efficient and comfortable. And third, the flatter, smaller saddles were more attractive, with a streamlined, clean, simple look, the better to show off our show hunters and equitation riders.

Chapter 4

~

Components of the
American Jumping
Style: Classical
Position

~

Mounting and Dismounting

Mounting is our first moment of actually riding the horse. Dismounting (on purpose or by accident!) is our last moment of riding for that day. Mounting correctly (or incorrectly) sets the tone for the ride; dismounting in a thoughtless way not only is dangerous but can affect the horse's attitude the next time you start to mount. Don't ever, ever forget that! Two of the most serious falls in my career have occurred during the dismount. Therefore mounting and dismounting, like everything we do with horses, have to do with safety first and efficiency second. Last but by no means least, they also have to do with feeling for the other guy, namely the horse.

Bill Steinkraus, a great friend and mentor, taught me never to get down onto a horse's back quickly or roughly. Ease down instead. After the toe has been placed in the stirrup iron and pointed into the girth, the rider steps up, places his right foot in the off stirrup, and *doesn't immediately sit down*. He slowly sinks down into the saddle and only gradually straightens up. Mounting a horse tells me pretty nearly the whole story about a person's attitude toward animals. This brief moment sets the whole tone of the American Jumping Style—soft and smooth.

(A wonderful book by Bill Steinkraus that I highly recommend is *Reflections on Riding and Jumping*.)

Basic Position

Once in the saddle, the rider picks up his reins in both hands and assumes his basic position. If he has to adjust his position (which happens over and over again during an hour's ride, no matter how expert the rider), he does it much like the final stage of mounting. He leans forward and stands up in his stirrups. This standing position, which we call two-point contact, makes it easier for the rider to weight his heels and come back into the center of the saddle, not the back of the saddle. This basic position is essentially the same for all North American riders, be they hunter, equitation, or jumper oriented.

Stirrup Length

In order to develop and maintain a good position and seat, you must be conscientious about stirrup length. Stirrups must be adjusted for what one is doing at a particular time. A good "rule of thumb" before mounting is to measure the stretched stirrup leather and iron from your fingertips at the stirrup bar to your armpit. This rough estimate is enough to ensure that the stirrups are at an approximately correct length, especially when mounting a green or difficult horse, where there probably won't be much time or opportunity to make adjustments once in the saddle. However, this method is not precise enough for most kinds of riding. A more accurate method is, once in the saddle, to stretch the leg down and feel where the stirrup iron hangs in relation to your ankle bone. For dressage riders, the iron should reach below the ankle bone; for all-purpose flat work, slow galloping, and low jumping, to the bottom of the ankle bone; for jumping bigger fences, to the top of the ankle bone; and for fast galloping and very big fences, just above the ankle bone. Stirrup length is critical to the rider's function. Too short a stirrup for the activity places the rider too high above the horse and can force him back in the saddle. Too long a stirrup is disastrous, as it robs the leg of its proper angles, elasticity, and security and leads to an insecure seat. Especially in jumping, it is better to ride a bit too short than too long. To constantly change one's length of stirrup every time there are changes in the activity can be a nuisance. However, for those who want to retain their style and effective position on a horse, it is the only way.

Stirrup Placement

Where does a rider's position begin? With the stirrup iron placed on the ball of the foot. Not only is the stirrup on the ball of the foot, but it is positioned in an exact way. Through the years we have refined every detail to produce this picture, which also proves effective in winning Olympic medals and World Cup Finals.

The foot is placed so that the little toe is at the outside branch of the stirrup iron, with the ball of the foot resting on the stirrup and the stirrup iron perpendicular to the girth of the horse. The stirrup tread crosses the ball of the foot at an angle; it is not perpendicular to the rider's foot. This is the softest, most flexible, and most natural place for the stirrup to rest, and it is also the most secure. If the stirrup were placed more toward the toe, the stirrup could easily be lost. When the stirrup is brought back behind the ball of the foot, toward the "home" position, the elasticity of the ankle joint is lost. The old French books tell you to put about one third of the foot into the iron; I'd say it is probably closer to one quarter of the foot for most people of the American School. Riding with just the tip of the toe on the stirrup is a useless mannerism; if you try it, you will probably lose your stirrups more often than necessary. In fact, when the going gets rough—in mud, rain, uneven terrain, or what have you—I bring my stirrups back a little farther on my foot for increased security.

Four Principal Parts
of the Body

There are four principal parts of the rider's body: the *leg*, from the knee down; the *base of support*, the thighs and seat; the *upper body*, all parts above the base; and the *hands and arms*. These four parts, when positioned correctly, enable the rider not only to have maximum security, but to maintain his balance at all gaits and when jumping. If the position of one of the parts is faulty, the rest of the rider's position becomes faulty as well. Therefore, the interrelation of these four body parts is extremely important.

The Leg: Position and Function

The *placement of the leg* is the foundation for the position of the entire body. The basic position for the leg is directly under the rider's body, with the stirrup leather perpendicular to the ground. When the leg loses its position and goes too far forward, the rider's seat and upper body will fall to the rear, which is likely to cause a loss of balance. This loss in turn can affect the hands, which then rely on the horse's mouth for balance. On the other hand, when the lower leg slips too far backward, the seat and upper body topple forward, putting the rider "ahead of the horse" and jeopardizing balance and control in the other direction.

Once the foot is perfectly placed in the stirrup, it is time to position the leg. This can only be done by standing up in the stirrups, leaning forward slightly out of the saddle (in what we call "two-point contact"), and driving the weight down into the heels. By displacing his weight (off his seat and buttocks and into his heels), the rider automatically drives his heels down. The heels, now the lowest point of the rider's body, act as a weighted anchor to give the rider great security in or even above the saddle. If the heels are kept down, not only is the leg stabilized and prevented from swinging around, but the muscles of the calf are made taut. These taut muscles give the leg its much needed power and grip. There is nothing more useless on a horse than slack calf muscles coupled with the rider's toes pointing down. This combination of errors causes a great lack of security, and the driving capability of the leg is also greatly diminished.

An educated leg lies from the knee down just behind the girth, with the heels down, the ankles flexed, and the toes out a little. The toes should not, as some people mistakenly believe, be perfectly parallel to the horse, and *definitely not* turned in. Both of these positions turn the lower leg out and cause it to swing, using the knee as a pivot. The toes should be turned out from fifteen degrees to forty-five degrees, depending on the rider's conformation. The lower leg should rest in light contact with the horse's ribs. We distribute the grip between the thighs, the inner knee bones, and the calves of the legs, never all in the knees. This position is what we call an "educated grip." The old-fashioned knee grip (and we were *all* taught it!) acts as a pivot, causing the lower leg to swing. We see a lot of this in Europe, both in dressage and in jumping.

An excessive grip in the lower leg (many beginners do this) is even worse. It acts as an involuntary driving aid, which can cause horses to run away if they tend to be "hot" in temperament or become dead to the leg if they are "cold" horses. A distribution of contact among the parts of the leg is what is wanted for an "educated grip," and hence an educated leg.

The Base of Support

The *base of support* includes all parts of the rider's body touching the saddle, namely the thighs and seat. There is not much to do with the thighs except to keep them physically thin and then to let them lie flat against the saddle, like a slab of raw meat thrown down on a table. The only way to keep thighs hard, strong, and fit is to do a lot of riding without stirrups. Nobody ever does enough riding without stirrups because we are all lazy! Riding without stirrups also happens to be the *only* way of developing and maintaining a really good seat, where the seat bones are able to stay connected to the saddle *no matter what the horse is doing*. Not only should the seat bones be able to "fix" to the saddle, but they should also follow the horse's movements at all times and in all gaits. This is a weakness of many riders in this country who ride hunters and equitation, but it shouldn't be! A faulty, weak, shallow seat is no part of the American Jumping Style.

The base of support should rest in the front/middle of the saddle. The rider is supported on his seat bones. If the buttocks slide to the back of the saddle, the rider's torso will fall forward and his legs will shoot out in front of him in a "broken stick" position. Not only will the seat be at fault, but so will the rest of the rider's body.

In a discussion of the base of support, it is important to understand that there are really two seats. In the American School, we refer to the "full seat," in which the rider is seated on the horse's back, as "three-point contact." The three points are the rider's two legs and his seat, which are all in contact with the horse. The term "two-point contact" is used to denote a "half seat" or a "light seat." The rider's seat is suspended off the horse's back while the seat bones and buttocks are very close to the saddle and can come into contact at a moment's notice; the only real contact between horse and rider exists in the rider's two legs. Two-point contact and three-point contact are aptly named and good riding language, facilitating easy communication and understanding. The other terms (full seat, half seat, and light seat) are also good ones; some teachers prefer these terms, and actually, I use all of them in my teaching.

When should we use two-point contact? In practice, only in the posting trot, when galloping on straight lines, during the flight of a jump, when riding uphill, and as an exercise. It is never used at any other time, and if used incorrectly it becomes a most faulty practice, where the rider gets ahead of the motion of his horse. In fact, good riders are in three-point contact (with the seat in contact with the saddle) most of the time while schooling their horses. The American School is a happy balance of "two-point" and "three-point," "up" and "down," and "with" and "behind" the motion.

We do use two-point contact frequently as an exercise. Standing up in the stirrups, holding the mane or a neck-strap for security, is by far the best and quickest way to develop a rider's leg position. It is also a great balance exercise, especially when the rider is at a stage where he does not need to hold the mane or the neck-strap. This "standing" exercise should be practiced at a halt, walk, trot, canter, and gallop, and while jumping low fences.

The base of support must never be neglected or underestimated. Not only does it provide support for the upper body, but it is also the focal point for all the aids (hands, legs, and weight) to work through. As such, it can be compared to the central telephone office. Much feeling concerning a horse is also transmitted to the rider through his seat. Those riders who have learned to really "sit" feel much more of what is going on than those who only stand up, both on the flat and over fences.

The Upper Body

The rider's *upper body*—all parts of his body above his base of support—is a good deal more flexible and changeable than either his leg or his base. There are many different positions or angulations for the upper body, depending on what one is doing on a horse. These angles are controlled by opening or closing the rider's hip angle—not at the waist or shoulders—while the legs remain in place under the seat. I have stated before, and it bears repeating, that it is impossible for the rider to have control over his upper body angulation if his legs are insecure.

At the halt, the rider's upper body is vertical—perpendicular to the ground over the horse's center of gravity. As the horse moves forward into a walk, both horse's and rider's centers of gravity shift slightly to the front, and so does the rider's upper body. The same thing happens at the sitting trot and the canter; the rider's upper body should be a couple of degrees in front of the vertical. However, for the posting trot, galloping, and jumping, it is necessary to close the hip angle even more and to lean forward up to thirty degrees, in order to stay with the motion of the horse and to have both horse's and rider's centers of gravity coincide. For the racing gallop (faster than eighteen miles per hour and ridden with very short stirrups), the center of gravity has shifted so much to the fore that the rider's upper body angulation increases to about forty-five degrees. We don't need this extreme forward position often except when galloping fast. On the other hand, bringing the upper body behind the vertical is occasionally useful when we really need to drive a horse forward or hold one back. The rider's weight is more powerful when moved to the rear, yet it doesn't pay to sustain this position for long because it gets in the horse's way. If the rider is perpetually behind or ahead of these correct positions, things will start to go wrong with other parts.

The most common faults of riders who ride constantly behind the motion are head jutting, roach back, ducking, jumping ahead of the horse, and dropping back over fences. These occur because the rider is constantly trying to catch up with his horse and, being behind the movement, is compensating. In the aforementioned cases, the head, shoulders, or whole upper body is trying to keep up with the horse. If these compensations are successful, form faults result; if they are unsuccessful, the rider drops back or, worse still, is left behind.

The *eyes* are part of the upper body, and eye control is of the utmost importance. When the eyes drop, balance, security, and coordination suffer. Nothing will work right! Only by looking up and ahead is one assured of good balance, coordination, and security in the saddle. The rider loses some of his feel when he looks down. Looking down is also a sure way to develop leaning problems and crookedness in the upper body, and it makes it impossible to ride a straight line or accurate turn. Probably the single most devastating blow to good style and good riding is for the rider to look down.

Other parts of the upper body include the neck, shoulders, chest, and back. The neck is held up and back, touching the rider's collar. The shoulders are relaxed and hanging down. The chest and stomach are "vaulted upward"—carried up rather than sagging or concave. The back is kept flat and the loins slightly concave. Too round and soft a back we call a "roach" back; too hollow and stiff a back is known as a "sway" back. In the "roach back" position, one tends to sit on the end of the spine and buttocks, so that some of the angulation of the upper body takes place at the waist instead of at the hip joint. In the "sway back" position, the rider tends to sit on his crotch, an even worse fault that puts the rider into a stiff, precarious perch ahead of his horse. Understanding the form and function of the upper body is terribly important. Not only is the correct position always more elegant, but by knowing how to use the back, principally by stretching the spine, we immediately become stronger and much more effective riders.

Hands and Arms

The *hands and arms* are the fourth part of the rider's body. The nuances of the hands and arms are so infinite that we never completely master all of their subtle and changing positions and feelings. The basic position, however, is relatively simple: form a classic straight line from the rider's elbow to the horse's mouth. This mandates that the "home" position for the rider's hands is slightly over and just in front of the withers, a couple of inches apart. The fingers are gently closed on the reins, in order to cultivate sensitive control. The little finger belongs outside the rein, and the thumb should be placed on top of the rein so that the rein doesn't slip. The hands should be about thirty degrees inside the vertical. This angle, similar to the angle of the bit in the horse's mouth, again reinforces the "straight line" principle, and a straight line promotes the most elastic, soft, and supple feel between hand and mouth. The wrist is straight, an extension of the forearm leading into the hand. The shoulders are relaxed and hanging down naturally, and the elbows are bent because they carry the hands.

With regard to hands and arms, there is nothing so important as establishing a straight line from the rider's elbow to the horse's mouth. Not only does this line provide the most direct, consistent, and elastic connection between the hand and the mouth, but it also prevents the hands and arms from forcing other parts of the body into faulty positions. For instance, when the rider lowers his hands too much, thus creating a broken line downward, what will happen? First, the shoulders are pulled down, and second, the back is rounded. As a consequence, the rider sits more on the back of his spine than on his seat bones, and his legs may even go forward. The rider's whole position and seat can thus be distorted by this one simple mistake of hands carried too low! A broken line upward (hands too high) will not, as a rule, affect the rider's body as a whole as much. However, this faulty position can be an indication of lack of independence of the hands, and that they are carried too high in an effort to aid in balance.

Violating the basic position of hands and arms will have its repercussions. Not only do hands consistently positioned below the horse's mouth (breaking the straight line from elbow to mouth downward) affect the rest of the rider's body, but such hands cause severe mouth problems with the horse. Any bit, when pulled downward, acts more severely on the sensitive bars of the mouth. A jointed snaffle, in addition to pressing downward on the bars, has a more severe "nutcracker effect" when pulled downward. Usually horses that are ridden with low, set hands tend to flip their heads or go above the bit in an effort to escape the constant pressure on the ultrasensitive bars of the mouth. The corners of the horse's lips are firm, rubbery, and more elastic; this is where most of the bit's pressure should be exerted.

High hands (a broken line upward, above the mouth) are not nearly so bad as too low hands, providing the hands are steady and smooth. These hands, as a rule, do not adversely affect the horse's mouth the way too low hands do. They tend to put more pressure on the corners of the horse's mouth instead of on the bars of the mouth. High hands also do not tend to cause as many problems with the rest of the rider's position. The problem with too high hands is that this habit indicates either a lack of control over the hands and arms, a lack of balance, or possibly both.

Flat hands (also called "piano hands" or "washboard hands") are too soft and weak. They are not as firm or effective as hands that lie thirty degrees inside the vertical. Another disadvantage is that flat hands can result in rounded shoulders and elbows out, affecting the rest of the rider's position and balance. Flat hands are often accompanied by partially open fingers. The rider has no real "feel" of the horse's mouth, and of course, he has less effective control. It is not necessary to ride with flat hands to be soft and sensitive.

Vertical hands—or, worse still, hands that are rotated with the thumb to the outside and past the vertical—are usually stiff. It has always been hard for me to remain elastic through the elbows and shoulders when my thumbs are straight up and down. Some people can do it, and of course, it looks very good, very classic. However, the best relationship with the horse's mouth—soft, supple, elastic, and effective —is about thirty degrees inward from the vertical position.

While it is best for the wrists to be straight as an extension of the forearm, they can flex a little to the inside. This bend gives some people a feeling of more elasticity. Cocking the wrists to the outside (or worse, downward) does the opposite—it locks the wrist and produces stiffness. Many riders have an unconscious habit of keeping one wrist bent more than the other all the time, which causes stiffness in one arm and can contribute to one-sidedness in the horse. Again, the principle of the straight line from elbow to mouth works best. This affords maximum control coupled with elasticity; we want and need both.

Any discussion of hands and arms must not forget the elbows. The elbow angle is one of the major angles of the rider's body; it is terribly important. This angle must be constantly flexible and "well oiled"; it must open and close automatically in movement with the backward and forward motion of the horse's head and neck. The elbow joints and, to a lesser degree, the shoulders act as shock absorbers between the rider's body and the horse's mouth. Shoulders and elbows must be soft, pliable, and elastic. "Soft arms" is a more accurate description than "soft hands." Stiff elbows will stiffen the entire rider, a stiffness quickly transmitted to the horse. Nor is it easy to feel or accompany the horse's stride with a stiff arm. Once the rider is "out of synch" with the horse's stride, it is impossible to see a distance or see a stride to a fence. Keep your elbows soft and you will be "with" the stride and "with" the distance. Need I say more about how important I feel elbows are?

Hands that are too far apart or too close together again violate the "straight line" principle. The hands should usually be two to three inches apart, although they sometimes can be a little wider when teaching a young horse to steer.

Remember that the hands close and the arms fix; they do not pull. There are numerous classical hand actions and rein aids which must be learned. Good hands and arms are within the realm of every rider.

There are many, many riders with bad (pulling) hands or "no" (ineffective) hands. Educated hands, those that know just how much pressure to apply and when to apply it, are a lifetime achievement.

When positioned correctly, these four principal parts of the rider's body—*leg, base, upper body, hands and arms*—enable one to ride in balance easily. Balance or equilibrium is terribly important; without it we are lost. If one part of our position is wrong, not only is it harder to ride in balance, but the error will affect other parts of the body and they will consequently go wrong. I have always believed that good form on a horse leads to better function, and that good function determines good form. Functioning correctly will tell you the truth about where the different parts of your body should be at different times; consequently, correct function puts you in position for good style.

Therefore, it is easy to see, just from a few examples, the interrelation not just between the four major parts of the rider's body, but also among small elements of each part and the whole. It is best to attempt a classic seat from the beginning. Classic form is not easily attained, and it is easier to lose. One form fault feeds on another. It is best when every individual part is maintained in as correct a position as possible.

The Angles of the Body

It is absolutely essential, when discussing, evaluating, or teaching style or form, to understand the angles of the rider's body: the ankle angle, knee angle, hip angle, and elbow angle. Once one knows about these angles, defining the rest of a rider's position is relatively easy.

The ankle angle, formed by the top of the rider's foot and his shin, stays closed, providing that the stirrups are the correct length. The heels remain lower than the toes, a position that keeps this angle relatively fixed. The angle should not open or close too much, although there is some flexibility.

The knee angle, created by the back of the calf and the underside of the rider's thigh, opens and closes. This angle is controlled by the thrust of the horse. When the rider is sitting in the saddle at the halt, rein back, walk, sitting trot, or canter, the knee angle, supple though it is, remains closed. Not so for posting the trot, galloping, and jumping. The fact that the rider is now out of the saddle part of the time causes this angle to open and close. But *it is the thrust of the horse, not an effort on the rider's part*, that causes the opening and closing of the knees. The rider should never consciously make an effort to open or close the knee angle. Meanwhile, the lower leg remains perfectly steady and in its proper position.

The next major angle is the hip angle, formed between the top of the rider's thigh and his torso. This major angle, unlike that of the knee, is controlled by the rider, not the horse. It is so important for a rider to practice opening and closing this angle, which is how he correctly leans forward and back. The American Jumping Style, essentially built around the Forward Seat, demands the proper use of the hip angle. To lean forward, the rider closes this angle, keeping his back flat, loins slightly concave, chest vaulted, shoulders relaxed, and head and eyes up. The rest of the body—legs, base, hands and arms—remains intact. The rider opens the hip angle principally by stretching his spine when he needs to make a transition to a halt or slower gait, or at moments when he needs maximum control. The hip angle cannot be effective in keeping the upper body in balance with the horse unless the legs stay securely in place, whether the hip angle is opening or closing.

The last of the angles, the elbow angle, is formed between the upper and lower arm. This angle both depends on and is determined by the line between the rider's elbow and the horse's mouth. It too is under the complete control of the rider. The lower the hands, the straighter the arms, and the more open the elbow angle; the higher the hands, the more the elbow angle closes. The elbow angle and height of the hands are influenced by the horse's head carriage, in order for the rider to maintain a straight line from the elbow to the horse's mouth. When the horse's head is carried low, the rider's hands must be lower and the elbow angle more open in order to maintain the desirable straight line. When the horse's head is high, the hands must be higher, and the elbow angle is more closed. For most of our work, however, the elbow angle will be about right when the hands are carried in the correct position just over and slightly in front of the withers, maintaining a straight line from the elbow to the horse's mouth.

Understanding, visualizing, and practicing the angles are all important. Without control of the four major angles of the body, good position and consequently style are virtually impossible. The indelible stamp of the American Jumping Style put on almost every American rider, old or young, is very much due to this emphasis on angles.

The Rider's Balance

The relationship between the four major parts of the rider's body and the correct angles of the body puts the rider in balance. If one part of the body is out of position, it is much harder to stay in balance—harder, but not always impossible. Acrobatic movements on horseback, especially over a jump, are an attempt (and often a good attempt) to keep one's balance. However, the educated artists who win today—Ian Millar, John Whitaker, Eric Navet—all are in perfect balance without being acrobatic. They are in a classic position.

There are three ways to ride a horse: "with," "ahead of," and "behind" the motion of the horse. No, I did not say "behind the horse," but behind the *motion* of the horse. Two of these ways are right —"with" the motion and "behind" the motion. ("Ahead of" the motion is used primarily as an exercise rather than a useful mode of riding.)

Why do we ride "with" the motion of a horse? The answer is simple: it is easier for both horse and rider. Due to its efficiency, it is usually smoother. The hip angle closes to an appropriate degree; the upper body angle shifts forward so that the rider's body mass is centered over the horse's center of gravity. In this position the rider does not have to catch up at a walk, trot, canter, or gallop, or over a jump. The horse moves or jumps, and the rider is right there "with" him, neither "ahead" nor "behind." The *sine qua non* of the American Jumping Style is riding "with" the motion of the horse. It is the stamp.

Why do we ride "behind" the motion? Simply because it is a stronger position from which to influence the horse. The upper body weight placed over the back of the seat and the buttocks adds more power to the rider's legs, his driving aids. Conversely, the body weight leaning back against the horse's mouth, coordinated with the hands and arms, makes the restraining aids through the reins and bit ever so much stronger. Riding "behind" the motion is not as easy as riding with the motion. It is only for good intermediate to advanced riders who have already acquired security, balance, coordination, and timing. If any of these qualities are missing, the rider will be "left behind" and will interfere with his horse's back, mouth, and movement—not only at a jump, but at a walk or trot as well. I have always felt strongly that my pupils should first learn to ride "with" the motion before attempting to ride "behind" the motion. Unless well done, riding "behind" the motion at worst can drastically interfere with the poor horse. At best, it can be rough and crude. Very few can do what Conrad Homfeld does:

to ride far "behind" the motion, catch up at just the right moment, and still always be smooth.

Riding "ahead" of the motion is usually relegated to an exercise today for riders who need to perfect their balance or who have a habit of riding too much "behind" the horse. It is very light and easy on the horse's back, so it can be useful when starting out on a cold-backed horse or a horse with an extremely sensitive back. However, the rider's balance placed more forward when riding "ahead" of the motion gives him less security and less effective control than when riding "with" or "behind" the motion. Some countries, namely Italy and Chile, used riding "ahead" of the motion as a system in former days. Today, the courses are too complex—with too sophisticated striding, turns, and angles—to permit riding "ahead" of the motion.

Due to our Thoroughbred influence, Americans have been forced to ride more or less "with" the motion of their horses. Thoroughbreds are, as a group, too hot and sensitive to stand a driving ride. Many if not all Thoroughbreds are especially sensitive in the back, and they react badly to the discomfort of being ridden too far "behind" the motion or, worse, being ridden by a rider who is left behind! We learned from them early on to lean forward by closing the hip angle, to stand up a little in two-point contact, and to lighten our seats. Yes, this is a compromising ride, but Thoroughbreds like compromise, and it works with them. Lightness, smoothness, and tact are the results. And for this reason the American Jumping Style is absolutely associated with riding "with" the motion in what is often termed the Forward Seat.

Use of the Eyes

One of the trademarks of style and elegance is the use of the rider's eyes. Eyes up and positive use of eyes produce good posture. The head is raised, the shoulders relax, the chest comes up and out. A straight yet relaxed posture and back is the wonderful result.

The use of a rider's eyes is one of the most important things in riding, especially in the American Jumping Style. It is too often neglected, both in riding a horse and in teaching people to ride. Consider driving an automobile: what would happen if the rider looked down at the steering wheel? He would crash into a tree! And it is much the same when riding a horse.

If we look down when riding, we don't necessarily crash into something, although we could. However, a lot of other things will go wrong. Take, for instance, balance. A rider who looks down tips his head down, and the head is a heavy weight at the top of his spine. This tipping can throw his entire upper body out of balance. With the rider's eyes up and ahead, his balance is so much easier to keep intact. Don't forget that balance and security in the saddle go hand in hand.

Coordination is another factor. We coordinate our balance, our aids, and all the parts of our body so much faster, even automatically, with our eyes up. Not so with the eyes down, for our coordination slows way down. And it is the coordination of our aids that counts, not the strength of our aids.

Direction too is affected. Riding lines and turns is virtually impossible without the correct use of eyes. American riders are taught to use positive control of their eyes by focusing on a specific focal point in line with a jump, and by shifting the focal point when turning. Eyes that wander aimlessly up and down, side to side do not permit clear direction. This eye wandering also causes large or small movements of the rider's head, which are felt by the horse and can cause him to wander aimlessly, too!

Timing, whether on the flat or over fences, also depends on correct use of the eyes. Almost everything else can be wrong, yet if the rider's eyes are "working," he will see the correct distance to a fence or make a transition at exactly the right spot. Looking down is fatal to good timing, and it's the best way I know to miss a distance.

All in all, eye control is basic to our total control over ourselves, our horse, and what we are trying to do. Just as in teaching other sports or learning to drive an automobile, we riding instructors "brainwash" our students in eye control in every lesson, right along with "Heels down," "Lean forward," and "Hands in line with the horse's mouth!" "Eyes up" belongs right here, and perhaps at the top of the list.

The phrase "eyes up" is rather too general to do or to teach. Style cannot be brought about by generalities; it must be produced by small, specific details. The positive use of eyes requires the rider to focus on a specific focal point. This point should be ahead of him in the exact direction he wishes to go, and at his eye level. It might be a tree, a post, a jump standard, or even his instructor, but it must be properly placed because he "aims" his horse directly at it. When the rider turns, he will shift his eyes to the next focal point. He must also look around his corners and look when crossing the diagonal of the ring. Then his horse will be more likely to go forward and straight. Believe me, that will fix most of the problems right there!

The rider must not let his eyes wander from his selected focal point. He mustn't look down if things go wrong, even if his horse bucks, wavers, or refuses at a fence. This is called "eye discipline," and it establishes the habit of keeping the eyes up and riding a positive line, no matter what happens. It keeps a rider organized, balanced, and confident, looking and thinking ahead.

Chapter 5

~

Components of the
American Jumping
Style: The Aids

~

Position and the Aids

Spectators the world over, be they other riders, trainers, or lay-men, "ooh and ah" about our beautiful style. This is due for the most part to two factors: position and use of the aids. Coupled together in the right way, this combination is a surefire recipe to produce a rider a cut above the average. Anyone can get around a course, and most people can even figure out how to have a clear round. The real artist is the Grand Prix winner who can go high, wide, and fast and still do it effortlessly with beautiful form.

Whether it be a rider's first time in the saddle or the day of the Olympic Games, he is learning, reviewing, or just subconsciously ad-justing his basic position. For to understand and to apply the aids correctly, we must have a correct basic position. If the seat, hands, or legs, or indeed any part of the body, is out of position, the rider will have to either apply his aids incorrectly or else move his hands, legs, or seat into the correct position when he needs to apply the aids. And we of the American School are not satisfied with crude, visible aids, especially for our hunter and equitation performances. Our aids must be quiet, subtle, and invisible for these divisions in order to satisfy the judges, our sensitive horses, and ourselves. Without invisible aids we'll go nowhere, and fortunately this philosophy becomes so embedded into our riding that it carries over into our work with jumpers.

The Driving Aids

The rider is settled into his saddle, his reins are short enough for him to have a feel of his horse's mouth, and his legs are in position on his horse's ribs just behind the girth. His natural aids—hands, legs, and weight—are already in contact with his horse. Now, to walk away from the stable to the schooling ring, he "applies the gas" by squeezing or closing his legs briefly against the horse's side. He *does not kick* with his legs. First, kicking compromises a rider's security in the saddle by taking his leg off the horse's side. Second, kicking only desensitizes the horse to the leg aid and makes him "dead to the legs." Third, kicking is a most crude and visible aid.

Rather than use a stronger, cruder aid like kicking, we learn to coordinate the driving aids together. The sequence is leg, cluck, spur, stick. On a sensitive horse, I can coordinate a cluck of the tongue with a squeeze of my legs and my horse will move off. The horse is trained to associate the cluck with a tap of a stick. If I do not get the response I want, I must resort to one of the artificial aids, my spurs or my stick. As I close my legs, I nudge my horse with my spurs at the same time, or if necessary I'll quickly but smoothly reach back and apply a stick behind my leg.

The spur is an accent to the leg, not a substitute for the leg. It is used with a brief inward nudge, never with a kick. There are variations of spurs to suit the sensitivity (or lack of it) of most horses. A few horses are so touchy and irritable that spurs can be counterproductive; if a stronger aid is needed, these horses do better with a stick.

The stick is the most powerful of the driving aids.* The mildest stick is a short bat with a flat popper that creates more noise than pain; the most severe is a long, stingy whip. Never apply a short jumping whip behind the saddle without taking your hand off the rein first; otherwise you will hit the horse in the mouth as you apply the stick, a classic example of clashing aids.

A clash of aids is when one aid contradicts another. The most common example is a leg that closes to ask the horse to move forward without the rider's hand first having relaxed and "opened the door." In the other direction are hands that close to ask for a backward response without the rider first making his legs passive. This clash can also happen in lateral work or in turning; for example, the right opening rein asks the horse to turn right, but there is no corresponding release with the left rein.

I've mentioned weight as a driving aid. Contrary to popular belief, it cannot be used alone, for if it is, it becomes almost powerless. However, by stretching the spine to weight the saddle while closing the legs, the rider makes his legs ever so much stronger. For the most part, it is better not to emphasize weight too much when riding or teaching riding. This emphasis can confuse riders, and it is best to allow the rider's weight to work automatically. For instance, in turning, just look in the desired direction; your weight will automatically do the right

* Anything stronger, such as unusual measures for rearers or very balky horses, is beyond the scope of this book—which, after all, is dealing with style! Anyway, most balkers and rearers, and sometimes even buckers, are started and pursued down this overridden road by uneducated riders who clash their aids.

thing to assist your turn. Consciously leaning to the left or right will be excessive and throw everything out of kilter.

As you can see, such a spectrum of driving aids can be coordinated so there is no need to use crude, rough, and visible aids to kick, pump, or "cowboy" your horse into moving forward. With this powerful progression of leg, weight, cluck, spur, and stick, and your understanding of how these aids work singly or in concert with each other, the horse should always be going forward and carrying himself easily in front of the rider at all times.

The Restraining Aids

Just as the brakes of an automobile are useful only when the vehicle is moving forward, it is only when the horse is going forward that the restraining aids are able to slow him down or stop him. Obviously the restraining aids must be clearly different from the driving aids, or else a clash of aids will occur. There is nothing worse than a clash of aids—it's the quickest way to sour and spoil a horse. From a safety and psychological point of view, I always teach beginners the simplest restraining aids before moving them out of a standstill. This is just good sense, and everyone is happier and more relaxed knowing something about stopping before they get started.

Our hands are our brakes and our steering. And our hands work just like our legs—they *close* but do not pull. Never use or think the words "kick" and "pull" if you want to learn to ride with the invisible aids associated with the American Jumping Style. The hands remain in position, neither raised nor lowered. They close much as in squeezing a sponge. When the horse responds, the fingers relax, but they do not open. Opening the fingers would drop the contact and allow the reins to slip through.

Again, the progression from lighter aids to stronger is simple. (All good riding is actually simple!) The arms are next in strength. The hands close, and then the arms "fix" in place, resisting any pull from the horse. Arms used in conjunction with hands are quite strong, but neither can compare with the use of weight. The rider's straightening up, stretching the spine, and sometimes even leaning backward against the horse's mouth can create restraining aids strong enough that few horses can resist. The weight of the rider's upper body thrown against the sensitive bars and corners of the horse's mouth is powerful indeed, so don't underestimate this tool! However, a good mouth is our objective if we want total control with invisible aids. To produce this mouth, we must understand the progression of natural aids: hands, arms, then weight.

The voice, principally the use of the word "whoa," is also a very helpful natural restraining aid. The horse must be trained to this aid through association with half-halts. (Don't use "whoa" too often in conjunction with a full halt, or someday he'll stop in front of a fence by mistake!) However, like the cluck, if the word "whoa" is relied on too much, it will become weak and ineffective. The horse must be frequently reminded through these associations that the voice means business.

Hands: Bad, "No," Good, Educated

There are four kinds of hands possessed by riders of different levels, sensitivities, and talents: "bad" hands, "no" hands, "good" hands, and "educated" hands. To understand riding and style, one must understand the difference.

We'll start with "bad" hands. Bad hands are hands that pull, jerk, or balance themselves on the horse's mouth. Beginners, in a sense, start off with "bad" hands. They have no security in the saddle and little balance at first, so they are apt to rely on the horse's mouth for both of these essentials. Most beginners also tend to pull while learning to control the horse. Fortunately, most beginners eventually progress, and their hands improve as they do.

Who else has bad hands? Rough, unfeeling, and uncaring "butchers" on horseback have bad hands. They are always abusing a horse's mouth by jerking and snatching. Unfortunately, these types, temperamentally unsuitable for riding horses, rarely if ever outgrow their bad hands. People who are "over their heads"—who are overmounted—may also have bad hands, a fact that instructors should remember. When someone gets left behind at a fence or involuntarily hangs on to the horse's mouth to save his balance, he too has bad hands. He may be neither a "butcher" nor a beginner; rather, he momentarily made a mistake.

Some riders, in an effort to develop "light" hands, have essentially "no" hands. Their hands are too limp, too light, and too ineffectual. These riders have no consistent contact with their horses' mouths. They often ride with open fingers, which allow the reins to slip through. "No" hands are not as destructive as "bad," pulling hands, but they are ineffective and can put the rider at risk. They are certainly not good hands!

"Good" hands are within the realm of *every* rider if he wants to learn. "Good" hands are steady hands; they do not bob up and down, and they most certainly do not rely on the horse's mouth for balance and support. To have good hands requires an independent seat; a rider who must sometimes hold on with his hands to keep his balance cannot have independent or good hands. He must also have good upper body, shoulder, arm, and hand position, and flexible arms and elbows.

"Good" hands have the ability to control the horse in a smooth, controlled way—to slow down, turn, stop, or rein back as needed and without pulling. They are well versed in all the rein aids and at least some of the rein actions. They are not yet expected to position the horse's head like "educated" hands. Their job is smooth, simple, basic control rather than the more advanced flexion and collection.

Very few people really acquire "educated" hands. (That is one reason so many people use draw reins so much!) Educated hands, by applying the exact degree of resistance to the mouth as the horse is resisting the hand, can flex the mouth, relax the jaw, and cause the horse to flex at the poll. This in turn allows the back to arch and the joints of the hindquarters to bend, permitting engagement of the hind legs. In other words, "educated" hands go a step further than "good" hands. They can do everything that good hands can do—slow down, stop, rein back, turn left and right, and execute all the rein aids. What's more, educated hands can use all the rein actions needed to place the horse's head and to influence his movement and balance. As I've said before, very few people ride enough horses long enough without the use of draw reins, chambons, or martingales to allow their hands to learn this skill. It takes a lifetime. Of all the thousands of people I've taught, I'd say only a handful really possess educated hands. Don't worry, though—for the purposes of learning, riding, or teaching the American Jumping Style, we need only concentrate on "good" hands. These will serve us well during the lifetime quest for truly "educated" hands.

The Rein Aids

(1)
direct rein
(turning)

(stopping)

(2)
opening or
leading rein

(3)
neck rein or
bearing rein

(4)
in front of
the withers

(5)
behind
the withers

indirect rein

The Rein Aids

In the American School, we are familiar and comfortable with the five rein aids, having been brought up on hot Thoroughbred horses that have plenty of impulsion and often need few or no leg aids at all. If we ride such horses, we must know how to ride almost exclusively with our hands.

Understanding these rein aids is very simple. Each rein aid is only a question of line from the horse's mouth backward or sideward, or both. In the first rein aid, the *direct rein*, the line is straight back from the horse's mouth to the rider's elbow. This rein is used for slowing, stopping, and turning. To stop or decrease pace, both hands close with equal pressure on the reins. For turning, one hand closes straight back, while the other relaxes forward. The horse turns his head slightly toward the active hand (the hand that closes) and turns in that direction.

A primary aid for turning—and indispensable for green horses and beginning riders—is the *opening or leading rein*. The rider's hand moves out to the side; the opposite hand gives and allows the horse to turn his head. The horse "follows his head" through the turn. In this rein aid, there is no backward pressure (unlike the direct rein), only sideways pressure.

Another very simple rein aid, often used in conjunction with the opening rein, is the *bearing rein or neck rein*. The active hand moves sideways against or even across the neck, withers, and shoulder, pushing the horse's forehand in the direction of the turn. This rein aid is very useful for speed turns.

The *indirect rein* is a combination of the direct rein and the neck rein. There are two indirect rein effects: one in front of the withers and one behind the withers. It is a question of line. The *indirect rein in front of the withers* goes from one side of the horse's mouth toward the *rider's* opposite hip. This rein aid not only bends the horse's head and neck slightly toward the same side, but also displaces his weight toward the opposite shoulder, thus balancing the horse for corners, turns, and canter departs. The *indirect rein behind the withers* has a subtle but most important difference. Coming from the horse's mouth through the rider's body toward the *horse's* opposite hip, it displaces weight from the inside shoulder to the opposite haunch. This rein is most useful for work on two tracks, such as shoulder-in and half pass. Another way to understand the difference between these two rein aids is that the indirect rein in front of the withers acts primarily sideways and a little backward, while the indirect rein behind the withers acts primarily backward and a little sideways.

The *pulley rein* is not one of the standard rein aids, but it is a practical one, with a substantial leverage effect. It is used most often in emergencies for control, or for stopping, slowing down, or turning on a

The Pulley Rein

galloping horse. To use it for stopping, the rider sets his inside hand down on the withers, while his outside hand comes up and back. This combination of hands lifts one side of the bit and turns the horse into the wall. For turns, the rider sets the outside hand on the withers and lifts the inside hand. I don't use this rein aid very much, as its crude leverage effect tends to make horses lean.

Rein Actions

The rein actions, which are different from the rein aids, coordinate with the rein aids. Besides the basic rein action of closing the hand, the rider's hands may "nip" or may alternate or vibrate the bit. There are infinite variations and combinations of active and passive pressure.

A *"nip"* or *jab* is a brief corrective action administered to a horse that lugs on the bit or roots downward with his head and neck. This discipline, used to lighten the horse that is heavy on the hands, is delivered in a short, upward action, usually with one hand, and is followed by an instant release and return to normal contact. Even beginners can learn this action; it helps to keep the horse's mouth responsive and is far more effective than pulling if a horse lugs, pulls, or tries to eat grass.

Vibrating or alternating the bit is a more advanced technique. The rider's hands slowly and smoothly alternate from side to side, the bit slides slightly in the mouth, and the horse yields in the jaw. Immediately on feeling this yield, the rider's hands must give and become steady. Personally, I've never had luck in teaching this very sophisticated technique to any but advanced riders. Most inexperienced riders don't vibrate the bit; they simply saw from side to side with their hands. Even worse, they may drop their hands and saw below the horse's mouth. This terrible sawing motion runs up through their arms and into their shoulders; sometimes even their upper bodies start rotating from side to side. All of this excess motion is rough and crude, and once acquired as a habit, it is hard to get rid of.

The rider's hand—like his leg or weight, for that matter—is either active, passive, or resistant. There is no other choice. When the hand acts, it closes. To make the hand stronger, the arm works with it by fixing itself to the rider's upper body. To make it stronger yet, the rider's weight moves back against the horse's mouth. This is the *active hand*.

The active hand increases pressure on the horse's mouth, while the *passive hand* lessens pressure. By relaxing the hand and arm (but not by opening the fingers!) toward the horse's mouth, the rider makes the hand softer and lighter. This is a yielding or giving hand. Oddly enough, most riders find it easier to "take" on a horse's mouth with an active hand than to "give" with a passive one; active hands seem to be more natural.

The most useful and yet perhaps the most elusive hand is the *resistant hand*, which requires understanding, feel, and patience. Why patience? Because one must wait for the horse. In using the resistant hand, one "fixes" the arm and hand and applies a certain amount of pressure. He neither increases nor decreases this pressure but rather waits for the horse to yield. Needless to say, once the horse yields to the "fixed" pressure, the hand also yields and becomes a passive hand. Horses tend to respond better in the long run to the resistant hand than the active hand; it is better for their mouths. However, one must constantly interchange among active, passive, and resistant hands to really put a sensitive, responsive mouth on a horse.

Lateral and Diagonal Aids

"Lateral aids" and "diagonal aids" are terms we should clarify to better understand, teach, and use the aids. While we really always use both hands and both legs when we ride, we are speaking here of which hand and leg are more active or dominant and which are, at the moment, more passive and supporting. I say "at the moment" because often the passive, supporting hand and leg become the active, dominant ones, and vice versa.

Lateral aids simply refers to both active aids (hand and leg) on the same side. For instance, when riding through a corner (the most basic of all bending lessons), the rider applies his inside rein and inside leg to bend his horse. Because the active rein and leg aids are on the same side, we call them "lateral aids." (To be even more specific, we could call them "inside lateral aids.") In this instance, the outside hand yields or becomes passive, allowing the horse to bend within reasonable limits. The outside leg goes back a little behind the girth, supporting the bend but remaining essentially passive. The dominant aids are the inside lateral aids.

Diagonal aids are active or dominant hand and leg opposite one another. For instance, diagonal aids for the left-lead canter depart would be an active left indirect rein in front of the withers, coupled with an active right leg. The inside (left) leg and outside (right) rein in this instance are passive or supporting aids. Again, they can become instantaneously active if necessary; the inside leg for more impulsion, and the outside rein to hold the horse next to the wall.

Inside Versus Outside Aids

The notion of "inside" versus "outside" aids is also important. Many riders are confused by this seemingly simple concept, especially when they encounter lateral work.

When one is riding in a ring, it is easy to identify the "inside" aids with the side of the horse toward the center of the ring, and the "outside" aids with the side toward the wall. When the horse bends around a turn, the correct bend is to the inside. For instance, when one is moving to the left ("on the left rein" is the technically correct term), the horse's left side is toward the center; the rider's left rein and leg are the inside aids, and his right rein and leg, toward the wall, are the outside aids. This concept is simple and clear in ordinary riding. However, when one is working in an open field or executing lateral work, "inside" and "outside" no longer have reference to the wall of a ring. To be more specific, they refer to the *bend of the horse's body*. "Inside" refers to the concave side, or the inside of the bend; "outside" refers to the convex side, or the outside of the bend. For example, if a horse is cantering on the right lead and bent to the right, the right side is the inside of the bend, and the rider's right leg and right rein are his "inside" aids; his left leg and left rein are the "outside" aids.

There are times when we may deliberately bend the horse toward the wall of a ring, executing a "counter-bend." This occurs in the counter-canter and in a shoulder-out. In these cases, the horse will be bending to the right even though he is moving to the left (or again, technically "on the left rein"). The "inside" aids will be the aids on the inside of the bend, not toward the center of the ring (in this case, the right leg and right rein). The "outside" aids are those on the outside of the bend: the left rein and left leg.

This concept is clear and simple, once it is understood. It is universally accepted in riding, whereas many things are not.

Coordination of the Aids

Aids act, support, and yield in coordination with each other. When they act against each other, as with a rider's closing his hands to stop while closing his legs to go, a clash of aids occurs. One of the cardinal sins in riding, especially with hot Thoroughbred horses, is to clash the aids. Asking a horse to do two opposite things at once results in confusion, frustration, and very often a fight.

First understand that your legs both applied at once mean "Go forward"; your hands both closing at once mean "Come back." Of course, there are a myriad of hand and leg aids and combinations thereof that have already been discussed, but at present, we are referring to the simplest commands.

Let's use a really green horse as an example, a three-year-old just starting to be ridden. A horse this green must be ridden with one aid at a time. Before applying the leg, we must completely yield the hands, even to the point of "throwing away" any contact with the bit. If we apply the leg without first yielding the hands, a horse at this level will not understand what to do. He will experience a clash of aids and may balk, back up, or even rear. It is the same when applying pressure with the hands to slow down or stop; the legs must first completely relax. A very green horse can understand only a leading or opening rein that leads him in the direction of a turn. A direct rein, indirect rein, or neck rein is beyond him and must be taught over time.

An older, more schooled horse is different. Because he has been conditioned through time and repetition to the different aids of the legs and hands, the rider does not need to totally yield or abandon one aid before applying another. He can tactfully combine aids, which is not the same as clashing them. His legs may close to prepare the horse for movement a fraction of a second before the hands yield and allow the horse to move off. His hands can close on the reins to maintain the horse's head carriage while his legs demand that the horse move forward to trot. His legs can also hold a little pressure as the horse slows down to halt, ensuring straightness and maintaining engagement. The horse now understands all the subtle nuances of the different rein aids and actions of the hand. Almost but not quite simultaneous coordination of the aids is the best way to communicate with the horse at this later stage; earlier on, however, this would have been impossible.

In short, the coordination of the aids is what really great riding is all about. Roughness, force, and crude, visible aids are not indicative of fine horsemanship. In fact, they are quite the opposite. Subtle, invisible aids, coordination, and "feel" are the hallmark of the good rider and of the American Jumping Style. Bill Steinkraus, an Olympic gold medalist and a living legend to jumping riders all over the world, proved that riding over fences was an art. How did he do this? By a lifetime endeavor to refine and coordinate his aids.

In conclusion, if we want to ride with invisible aids—the *sine qua non* of stylish riding—we must have a detailed understanding of every aid, its purpose, and its use. Also, it is impossible for the horse to carry himself and respond to the rider in a smooth, effortless manner unless he is "at the aids." Therefore, the horse must be schooled to be as responsive as possible to the least amount of leg, weight, and hand, which are coordinated with the artificial aids of spurs, stick, and martingale as necessary. It is up to the rider to teach the horse to carry himself and his rider. The horse must do the work. The rider must never do more work than the horse. Otherwise there is no chance for beauty, art, and style.

Chapter 6

~

Work on the Flat

~

General Considerations:
Calm, Forward, Straight

It is virtually impossible to develop any system or style with a jumping horse without first having a comprehensive understanding of how to work a horse at the walk, trot, canter, and gallop. Again we have to thank the standard demanded by our hunter and hunter seat equitation divisions for the perfectionism Americans have learned to put into their flat work. A rider's position, use of aids, and understanding of flat work should blend together, whether the rider is a "first grade" beginner or a "college level" Olympian. What we are seeing today in hunter, equitation, and even jumper performances is almost "dressage over fences." This does not mean a dressage seat over fences, but the refinement of position, invisible aids, and smooth but precise control during a jumping round. And this carryover into the show ring is impossible without a mastery of work on the flat.

Surely the first principle to understand is impulsion. One of the cornerstones of the American School is impulsion—horses carrying their riders by moving and thinking forward. Impulsion is a moral quality as well as a physical one; the horse must think forward, and calmly but instantly move forward, whether moving straight forward, moving laterally, or even halting and reining back.

Impulsion begins with the first step forward. After the rider settles into the saddle, picks up the reins, and assumes his basic position, does the horse truly respond to the legs and move forward? Very rarely when I get on a new horse, even those ridden by great and famous riders, do I get this initial response. In the American School, we do not believe in working to make a horse go forward. If he does not respond to a slight squeeze or closing of the calf, the stick or the spurs are applied. The horse learns to associate the leg, cluck, spur, and stick with impulsion or forward movement. Without this response, and without our really understanding impulsion, it is impossible to ride and jump smoothly with invisible aids.

Obviously, unchanneled impulsion is useless. There must be control, and control comes from the hands, especially from the half-halt. The rider's closing his hands makes the horse slow down, halt, or rein back. This is how simple the half-halt is. The half-halt is responsible for regulating the pace and rhythm and balancing the horse. A horse that doesn't listen to the hands is actually a dead-mouthed runaway, even if he is only at a walk. The horse's primary response to the legs and, secondly, to the hands is what riding is all about. Other exercises, which are relatively easy, are designed to make the horse better, softer, and more responsive to the "gas pedal" and to the "brakes."

Once the horse is in front of the legs and behind the hands, so to speak, we want to make him straight. There are many ways to make him straight: the hands alone (which control the forehand); the legs alone (which can control the forehand when used at the girth or control the haunches if used behind the girth); or the hands and legs together, which is what we do most of the time. The simple goal of straightness is to line up the haunches with the shoulders so that the horse "tracks straight"—the left hind leg follows the track of the left fore, and the right hind leg "tracks" the right fore. With regard to the straightness of the horse's spine, the axis of the neck and back should be as straight as an arrow when the horse is traveling on straight lines and curved crescentlike when traveling on a bent line. A "straight" horse is one that tracks straight, but paradoxically, a "straight" horse in a turn must be bent in accordance with the turn, to keep his hind feet tracking accurately behind the forefeet.

Once we understand the simplicity of the directive phrase "Calm, forward, straight," and we grasp that the only *real* goals of riding are to be able to go forward, come back, and turn left and right as smoothly and rapidly as possible, we can proceed to work the horse on the flat in a productive way. (To understand these concepts is simple; to accomplish them can be quite complex!) By "productive" I mean to improve the horse's rideability over fences. Any dressage work that doesn't relate directly to improving the horse's mental or physical condition, or to making him easier to gallop or jump, should be discarded.

The object of any dressage is to train the horse. What we call schooling jumpers is the same as dressage over fences. I personally feel that our training of horses both on the flat and over fences through the American Jumping Style is often more pure and simple than the training that is often found at dressage shows. We too need a relaxed, supple, yet impulsive horse at one with his rider. Our horses must be submissive yet totally relaxed about their riders and their work. Any tension will cause distraction, and this lack of concentration is what causes horses to knock down fences. A gradual, necessary progression of training is what we are after. Anything forced or hurried will physically and mentally damage the horse, rider, or both—probably forever.

Lightness and self-carriage are essential to the American Jumping

Style. Horses characterized by freedom and regularity of pace, ease of movement, straightness, and bending, along with a lightening of the forehand and engagement of the hindquarters, represent the way our horses must be trained and must perform. This confident attention, so very apparent in the show ring, is impossible to produce without three good basic gaits: a regular, free walk; an active, energetic, regular trot; and a cadenced, light, and united canter that becomes a relaxed, supple, loose jumping gallop. As I've said before, *impulsion*, the instantaneous response of the horse to the rider's legs, is the cornerstone of all control through the various aids. This impulsion, of course, comes to the horse most naturally when galloping.

Impulsion or forward movement, coupled with flexion of the mouth (that is, the horse yielding his jaw to one or both reins), allows the rider to ride his horse "on the bit." Characteristics of a horse truly "on the bit" start with the horse's hocks, which should be under the horse, not out behind. The second characteristic is the arch of the neck. The horse should flex at or just behind the poll, not somewhere in the middle of the neck. Thirdly, the horse must be straight between the rider's seat, legs, and hands. He should not avoid the aids behind, to one side of, or even ahead of the rider. The horse accepts the contact of the rider's hands with a correctly placed and steady head carriage. Most important of all is not the *look* of a horse "on the bit," but rather the *feel*. Never should a riding or jumping horse be leaning on the hands, pulling the rider's seat out of the saddle, or throwing the legs away from his rib cage. Self-carriage requires the acceptance of the rider's aids and of *all* contacts—leg, seat, and hands.

Hunters and jumpers working on the flat must be schooled as well as their conformation and temperament allow. Regularity and activity of rhythm perhaps come first, but there are other things as well. Suppleness and smoothness, coupled with correctness in all the exercises and a prompt, relaxed obedience, are just as important. Of course, each horse is built differently and has a different temperament, all of which must be taken into account, especially when putting him "on the bit." We cannot force a horse into a mold, which is where soft, smooth, invisible aids and equestrian tact come in. (And these, as we've said before, depend upon the rider's natural, correct, and classical position.) These aids are effective, but they do not offend the horse, the rider, or the onlooker. This application of and response to the aids is one of the main goals of the American School.

The Gaits

One of the first things I teach riders about gaits is the approximate rate of speed for each gait. A sense of the evenness of pace is thereby established early on, and it is so instilled as to become habitual later on when jumping a course. The ordinary walk of a sixteen- to seventeen-hand horse is approximately four miles per hour; the collected sitting trot, six miles per hour; the ordinary posting trot, eight miles per hour; and the canter, ten to twelve miles per hour. For the extended or collected aspect of any gait, just give or take one or two miles per hour upward or downward. A hand gallop (the jumping gallop) is fourteen to sixteen miles per hour, while a hunting pace is approximately eighteen miles per hour. Anything over eighteen miles per hour is considered a racing gallop, the kind of gallop we often use in jump-offs and speed competitions against the clock.

Along with a gait's speed, riders must become aware of its rhythm. The walk is a four-beat gait and is characterized by a "restless" quality. The trot is an energetic yet regular two-beat gait with suspension or "bounce." The canter, which often has more natural impulsion than the other two gaits, must be controlled and cadenced into a regular three-beat gait with suspension. While the gallop is actually a four-beat gait, it seems as if there is really only one beat per stride once the horse is established in the gallop; it feels and even sounds like the beat of a drum. There is a pulsating quality when galloping down to one of those massive Hickstead or Aachen fences. Calmness, forwardness (or impulsion), and straightness are intrinsic qualities that should be present in every gait, even the fastest gallop.

Riders of the American School are educated to work equally on both diagonals at the trot and both leads at the canter, to ensure that no one-sidedness creeps into their horses' development. American riders post on the outside diagonal; that is, they rise and sit simultaneously with the horse's outside foreleg and the inside hind leg rising and falling. The diagonal is changed when changing directions.

Besides the ordinary and working walk, trot, and canter, there are the collected and extended modes of each gait as well. Because of the progression in schooling a horse, each gait has a medium mode called "lengthening the stride" between the ordinary and the extended gaits. The working gaits are a medium mode between the ordinary and the collected gaits. When riding on long or loose reins at the walk, we are executing a free walk. Riding on loose reins is a good exercise at the trot, canter, gallop, and jump also, and it is part of schooling in the American Jumping Style.

Along with the gallop, the canter is the gait we use most of the time for jumping, and it can therefore be considered the most important of all gaits for the jumping horse and rider. In order to really control, supple, and balance the horse at the canter, there are several exercises that must be practiced: counter-canter, the simple change of lead, and the flying change of lead. In the counter-canter, the horse is on the outside lead, deliberately on the "wrong" lead. To be in correct balance, he must be bent to the outside, toward the leading leg. This particular exercise collects and balances the canter, and as such, it is one of my personal favorites.

Another good collecting exercise is the simple change of lead. It automatically collects the horse by virtue of the downward transition involved in bringing the horse back to the walk before striking off on the new lead. There should be two or three clearly defined walk steps between one lead and the other. On a green horse, this exercise is done with several steps of sitting trot between leads, as changing leads through the walk would demand too much collection for the horse at that level. Besides enhancing collection, the simple change of lead promotes perfect obedience to the canter depart, the strikeoff into the canter.

The flying change of lead at the canter is probably the single most important exercise for the jumping horse. Clean flying changes are a necessity for smooth, fast, and well-balanced changes of direction at the canter or gallop. A horse with a natural aptitude for the flying change is easy to school. Horses that do not come by flying changes naturally are at best difficult to show, and at worst, in extreme cases, impossible to show—especially in the hunter and hunter seat equitation divisions, where clean flying changes are expected. A cross-canter or disunited canter often occurs when a horse fails to change leads in both front and hind legs. In a hunter or hunter seat equitation performance class, a cross-canter is of such major concern that it virtually eliminates the contender. In a jumper class, cross-cantering can disrupt the horse's rhythm, distance, and balance, especially on a turn, to the point of forcing a rider to pull up or circle before a fence.

The important elements in executing the flying change are (1) straightness, with the horse bent slightly toward the new lead; (2) regularity of pace, so the horse is not going faster or slower during the change; and (3) response to the rider's outside leg aid, as the horse moves his quarters slightly away from the rider's leg aid and conse-quently changes leads behind. In my opinion, a jumping horse cannot ever be too well schooled in flying changes. They should become auto-matic in turns, easy on straight lines, and even possible on a circle or in a series on a straight line. Some of my best jumpers have been able to do flying changes at every other stride and even at every stride, al-though this skill is not really necessary.

The importance of halting is often underestimated in the school-ing of horses. I believe in doing lots of halts when working on the flat and also when schooling over fences. I want my horse to stop obedi-ently, smoothly, and promptly from my restraining aids of hands, arms, and weight. When I close my hands, sink into the saddle, and stretch my spine, my horse must instantly halt. While at the halt my horse should stand immobile, square, and straight. He should not back up, swing his haunches, or look to the left or right. The rider's legs hold the engagement and maintain the straightness during the halt, doing nothing more. The great benefit of halts is that they prepare and also perfect the horse's response to the half-halt.

The term "half-halt," complicated as some might make it, simply means to slow down. The half-halt is obtained in the American School by the rider's hands, reinforced if necessary by his weight. Again, all the rider's legs need to do in a half-halt is to ensure straightness and engagement—to see that one does not lose the horse's hindquarters to the side or to the rear while slowing down. Except for the horse's response to the rider's legs, there is nothing in riding so important as the response backward to the rider's hands—the half-halt. Half-halts should be practiced continually to secure balance, collection, and con-trol. They are used to gain a horse's attention before attempting any new lateral or longitudinal movement.

The rein back, or backing up, is simply a continuation of the half-halt and the halt. The horse moves backward away from the rider's hands, which are reinforced if necessary with his weight. The legs simply maintain the horse's straightness in the rein back. There is no need for a strong leg. The horse should step back smoothly, regularly, and promptly on a straight line, and after completing the desired number of steps, he should then move forward instantly in response to the rider's legs. The rein back can be a powerful tool to soften the horse to the halt and half-halt. All of these movements should be thought of together as training the horse to listen to the rider's hands.

Transitions, or changes of gait and speed, are in a sense tied in with the halt, the half-halt, and the rein back. Transitions help to render the horse lighter to the legs and lighter to the hands. There are transitions upward (forward) and downward (coming back) within a gait and from one gait to another. First, a transition must be smooth; second, it must be prompt. It is important to maintain the rhythm or cadence of a gait during transitions—especially downward transitions, where the impulsion and activity can be lost—and to establish the rhythm of the new gait when making transitions from one gait to another. No matter how simple making a transition seems, it is often difficult to do perfectly, with the horse remaining in front of the legs and light to the hands, and with his head in a perfect position. Try it!

The highly balanced gaits, the passage and piaffe, are not necessary for a show jumper. However, done in moderation by someone who knows what he is doing, they certainly can't hurt a horse and could possibly make the horse jump better by developing his hind end. The passage is the most collected trot, and also the most measured, elevated, and cadenced. The piaffe is essentially the same; however, this most collected trot is done in place, nearly on the spot. The big difficulty in both of these exercises is to collect or slow down the trot to this point without losing impulsion and, as a result, the rhythm. Consequently, this exercise at the trot, requiring the coordination of seat, leg, and hands, really could only be good for both horse and rider as long as the movement does not become overvalued for itself.

Turns and Turning Figures

What is really important for the jumping horse and rider to master in daily work is turns and turning figures. In these figures the horse must follow the rider's aids explicitly; such obedience is absolutely essential in riding against the clock. Flexibility and bend of the horse from head to tail in the direction of the turn are musts, with the horse following the track of the turn with his hindquarters in line with his shoulders.

Corners are the most fundamental of all the turning figures. The horse must follow the track of the corner and be bent to the inside without hindering the free, forward movement of the pace.

The following are some of the turning figures that every well-trained horse and rider should practice. A simple *turn* or *corner* is a 90-degree turn to the right or left. The scope of this turn can vary from a shallow turn of several degrees to a 360-degree full *circle*. A *volte* is a circle six meters in diameter; any larger circle is simply termed a "circle." The *change through the circle* is a change of direction; it looks like an S turn with one straight stride at the center, executed through the center of a circle. A *serpentine* (a great figure for jumping horses) is a series of half circles connected by a short, straight line across an imaginary center line; the rounded loops should be of equal size. The *figure of eight* (another of my favorites, both on the flat and over fences) consists of two circles in opposite directions connected by a short, straight line. Obviously, the bend of the horse and the diagonal at the posting trot

Schooling Figures (1)

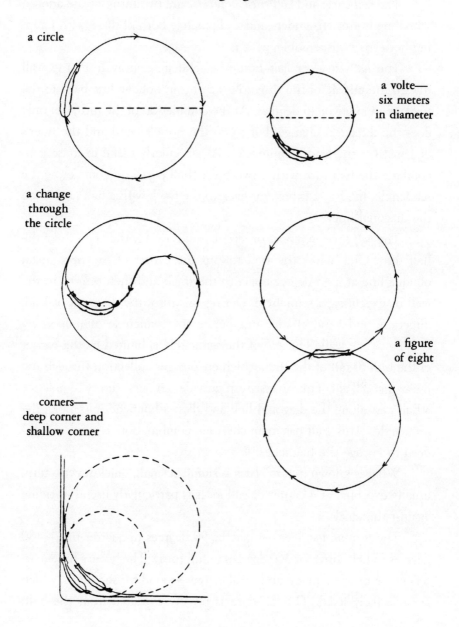

a circle

a volte—
six meters
in diameter

a change
through
the circle

a figure
of eight

corners—
deep corner and
shallow corner

(or the lead at the canter) will change with each change of direction, except when the counter-canter is executed.

The *half circle* and *half circle in reverse* are two turns we use a lot in schooling horses. To understand and practice both of these with jumping horses is indispensable, as it is in dressage.

The *half circle* or *half turn* is a semicircle away from the wall toward the middle of the ring, followed by an oblique line back to the track at an angle of 45 degrees. At the completion of the turn, not only does the direction change, but so do the horse's bend and the rider's diagonal (or the lead if cantering). A particularly useful exercise is to combine the half turn with a two-track (half pass); on completing the semicircle, the horse is brought back to the track with a half pass along the diagonal line.

The *half circle in reverse* or *reverse turn* is simply the opposite of the half turn. One leaves the wall toward the center of the ring on an oblique line at a 45-degree angle to the track and then returns to the wall by executing a semicircle. During this turn, the diagonal or lead, direction, and bend change just before the semicircle, not upon returning to the wall. The size of the semicircle is limited by the barrier of the wall or rail of the ring, which encourages collection through the use of a visual aid. This reverse turn provides an opportunity to practice a half pass along the diagonal line and then a haunches-out along the semicircle. This half-pass/haunches-out combination is powerful indeed to engage the haunches.

What is known as a *roll-back* is simply a small, quick reverse turn, usually executed at a canter or gallop. It is particularly useful in riding against the clock.

The *turn on the forehand* may be 90 degrees (a quarter turn), 180 degrees (a half turn), or 360 degrees (a full turn). The horse's hindquarters move in even, quiet, and regular steps around his shoulders, which are relatively fixed. This exercise is usually executed from the halt;

Schooling Figures (2)

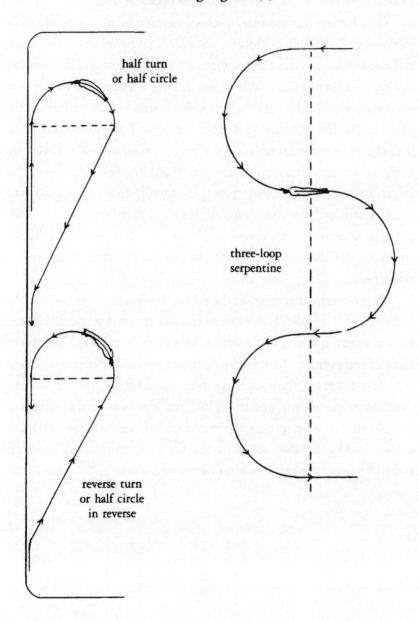

half turn
or half circle

three-loop
serpentine

reverse turn
or half circle
in reverse

however, it is good for suppling to do it from the collected walk. In elementary work, the horse is bent toward the rider's active leg; in advanced work, the horse is bent in the opposite direction.

The *turn on the haunches*, a schooling exercise also done from the halt and from the collected walk, not only is preparation for the pirouette but also is directly relevant for quick jumping turns. The same use of aids, coordination, and subsequent feeling is present as in the turn on the forehand. The hind legs describe a small circle or half circle, while the forehand turns on a larger circle or half circle around the haunches. For this turn to be done correctly, the horse should be bent in the direction of the movement and should remain active with his inside hind leg—he does not pivot. Eventually this turn should take place nearly on the spot, without losing the rhythm of the walk, through 90 degrees, 180 degrees, or 360 degrees. Impulsion and rhythm are musts; for the hindquarters to deviate backward or sideways is a major fault.

The *pirouette*, executed at the canter, is similar to the turn on the haunches at the walk. This movement is of course a wonderful lesson for the jumping horse, because it relates directly to very short speed turns in competition. During the pirouette or half pirouette, the horse must first maintain the canter rhythm; second, he must bend in the direction of movement; and third, his hind legs must turn as closely as possible to the same spot as is possible for his degree of collection. A well-trained horse, when asked for this turn, will truly "carry" his rider and will pirouette almost as if on his own.

Lateral Movements

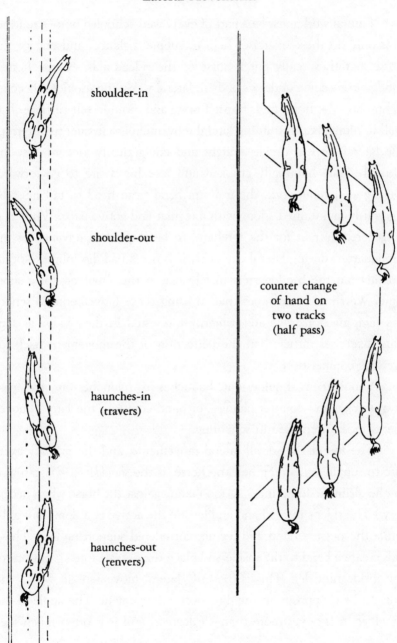

shoulder-in

shoulder-out

haunches-in
(travers)

haunches-out
(renvers)

counter change
of hand on
two tracks
(half pass)

Lateral Work

Lateral work must be a part of every well-schooled horse's routine. Not only do these exercises help to supple, balance, and engage the horse, but they really put a horse to the rider's aids. As the horse's hindquarters come under its body in lateral work, the shoulders become lighter and the horse finds himself more and more in self-carriage. It is well to remember in training lateral movements to frequently interrupt the lateral work and ride straight and energetically forward, lest the horse become habitually crooked and lose his desire to go forward. During all lateral work, the uniform bend from head to tail must be rigorously maintained, along with a regular and active pace. While it is considered correct for the forehand to be slightly in advance of the hindquarters during lateral exercises, it is not a bad discipline to occasionally put the hindquarters in advance of the shoulders for a short time. We should remember that in using these movements to school the jumping horse, we are primarily interested in their value as suppling exercises rather than the perfection of the movement itself for dressage competition.

Shoulder-in, shoulder-out, haunches-in, haunches-out, half pass (two-track), and counter changes of hand comprise the lateral movements most often used in schooling.

The foundation of all lateral movements, and the primary exercise to supple and strengthen the horse, is the *shoulder-in*. (It can also be the ultimate disciplinary action taken against the horse when necessary.) The rider's inside hand and leg are the active and dominant aids, while the outside hand and leg are considered supporting aids. These aids create a bend to the inside and place the outside foreleg in front of the inside hind leg. This is the only lateral movement in which the horse is bent opposite to the direction of movement. The angle of the shoulder-in is never more than 45 degrees, and it is often much less;

the angle and the degree of bending at any given time depend on the amount of lateral suppleness the rider wishes to obtain.

The *shoulder-out* is exactly the same as the shoulder-in, except that the horse is bent to the outside. The shoulder-out movement to the left is the same as the shoulder-in to the right: the aids are the same and the purposes are the same. However, more time should be spent in shoulder-in to reinforce bending to the inside.

Haunches-in (also called *travers*) is a more advanced movement than shoulder-in because the horse must understand the diagonal aids (that is, leg and rein aids on opposite sides) and must bend in the direction of the movement. This exercise is even more powerful than the shoulder-in in controlling and engaging the hindquarters. The horse follows the track with his shoulders and brings his hindquarters to the inside. The whole horse remains bent around the rider's inside leg and moves on two parallel tracks—shoulders on one track and haunches on another—at an angle to the track which never exceeds 45 degrees. The outside legs cross and pass in front of the inside legs, and the horse bends and looks in the direction of the movement. The haunches-in can be executed on a straight, circular, or diagonal track.

Haunches-out (also known as *renvers*) is simply the reverse of haunches-in. The horse's head and tail are turned toward the wall; everything else remains the same. I almost prefer haunches-out to haunches-in, especially for the early training of these exercises. The great advantage of haunches-out over haunches-in is that the horse is constantly turning his shoulders away from the direction in which the rider is asking the haunches to go. It is therefore impossible for the shoulders to "creep" in the same direction as the haunches, which is always a problem in the training of haunches-in. The bend, of course, must be rigorously maintained, but this time toward the outside.

The *two-track* (or *half pass*) is executed on the diagonal of the arena. The horse maintains his bend in the direction of the movement, faces forward (parallel to the wall), and moves forward and sideways at a 30- to 45-degree angle. His movement must stay rhythmic, active, and lively. He moves on two distinct tracks, with the outside legs crossing over in front of the inside legs, and his forehand always a bit in advance of the hindquarters. A *counter change of hand* is a zigzag maneuver in which the horse moves on two tracks alternately to the left and right, with a moment of straightness between changes of direction. To execute a two-track, a counter change of hand, or a broken line on two tracks is one of the marks of a very well-schooled horse.

A Note on Bitting, Tack, and Equipment

Bitting and tack for flat work in North America, on the whole, is generally simpler than that found in many other countries. We've found, much like the purists of classical dressage, that working through most problems on the flat with only the simple, smooth jointed snaffle is the best way to go. Of course, there are lots of people and certain horses that don't do it this way, and that is their prerogative. Although there are (hopefully) fewer side reins, draw reins, chambons, extreme bits, and the like in North America, there are still many more, mind you, than there need to be or than I'd like to see.

My personal preference, which I use every day on every horse in my stable for basic dressage work, is a smooth, jointed full-cheek snaffle. While this is not an extremely thin snaffle bit, it is not of the very thick variety either. Horses often tend to lean on very thick bits just a little, even with very good riders, causing both horse and rider to have to pull too much. I like full-cheek bits for the obvious reasons: the bit can never slide through the horse's mouth, and horses turn better with the pressure of the full cheeks. I do not own a pair of draw reins. The job of positioning the horse's head belongs to the rider's hands, not to an auxiliary rein. Riders will never really develop educated hands as quickly or as well while allowing themselves the crutch of using auxiliary reins. These reins don't hurt the horses particularly; rather, they hurt the rider's progress.

As far as bitting for galloping, jumping, and showing is concerned, I have one simple rule of thumb: *whatever works!* Very few horses work and jump at speed, especially in the "heat of battle" that is competition, in just a plain snaffle and still manage to stay light. Yes, some do, but many do not. And the ideology that I have imparted for many years now in North America is to try to do as much as possible on the flat in a plain, smooth snaffle, so that when the horse and rider go to fast work (galloping and jumping), we have somewhere still to go in increasing the severity of the bit. We may increase the bitting just a degree (a soft twisted snaffle, for instance), or we may go all the way to a kimberwicke, gag, or elevator bit.

I have nothing whatsoever against martingales. The only two types of martingales seen as the norm in North America are standing and running martingales. German and Irish martingales are used, but they are rare indeed. All or nearly all of our hunters are shown in standing martingales. A hunter judge would only penalize the entry if the martingale were too short. Our standing martingales are usually adjusted so that, if one pushed the strap up toward the horse's throatlatch, it would almost but not quite touch it. A horse must not be "tied down." Too short a martingale limits him as an athlete and causes stiffness. Let's face it—all a martingale does, be it standing, running, or German, is to limit how far a horse can throw his head. Its first purpose is to see that the rider is not hit in the face by the horse's head; its second is to keep the head within a certain range so that the hands can influence the mouth and "come through" the horse. In no way can a martingale be considered a training aid for the mouth. Rather, it is a stopgap so that the hand and the bit can better work the mouth. More and more horses and riders of the American School are going with no martingale at all. We've finally realized that it is the hand and the brain that really count. Martingales, in the overall scheme of things, are a minor aid.

Americans are very aware of the dangers of a too short running martingale. In fact, we are almost paranoid (and rightly so!) about correctly adjusting this type of martingale, so that the rings, when stretched up by the rider's hand, run up to the withers. Why are we so sensitive to a running martingale not being too short? You must re-member that we have grown up around the Thoroughbred horse, a horse which is sensitive, delicate, and thin-skinned. When a too short running martingale is hanging constantly on the supersensitive bars of the horse's mouth, the horse, to escape this painful pressure, will throw his head higher. A running martingale aids in framing the horse, but it in no way holds the head down. Once the horse is afraid of this con-stricting aid, his head will go higher, his back hollows out, and the price will be paid in his hind end. You'll start having faults behind—especially with a thin-skinned, hot Thoroughbred-type horse, but actu-ally with any horse.

Nosebands are something else again. We have come to accept different types of nosebands more recently, perhaps in the last thirty years. Our hunters must show in regulation cavessons without dropped noseband attachments. This, of course, is a test of mouth and manners. However, part of the show jumper's equipment today, and therefore part of the American Jumping Style, is a supplementary noseband—either a dropped noseband, a figure-eight noseband, or a "flash" nose-band (a dropped noseband attachment connected to a regular caves-son). Because the noseband prevents a horse from opening his mouth to evade the bit, a good percentage of the resistance is automatically eliminated. Horses' mouths can improve instantly and dramatically when one attaches this little strap. While a noseband should not be loose and sloppy, it should not be too tight either, or else the mouth cannot flex and "champ" the bit. One should be able to slip two fingers (snugly) between the horse's chin and the leather.

As far as saddles are concerned, we in North America have preferred the Italian Pariani and (later) the French Hermes saddles for years. We have always preferred flat, light, "close contact" saddles to the bigger, padded, and deeper-seated saddles favored by the continental schools of riding and jumping. This preference evolved for two reasons. First, we have always ridden and preferred the Forward Seat over the dressage seat for most of our riding endeavors. And second, we like to be close to our horse physically, getting a more intimate feel of what is going on between our legs and under our seats. Our emphasis on lower leg contact and the overpadded "basket" type saddle are contradictory. Therefore, it's the flat "close contact" saddle for us, with a minimum of knee roll, thigh roll, panels, and padding. Saddles must be compatible with style.

A jumping whip and a pair of spurs are more than just an accepted part of the American Jumping Style; they are almost mandatory. Any well-balanced regulation-length whip will do, but the whip should not be so short as to be merely a toy. For the "cold" horse, or a horse with a balk or stop, a longer, stingy whip is needed. However, the look of this more severe aid does not enhance one's style; rather, it detracts. The whip should blend in with the appearance of horse and rider. It should not draw attention to itself because of its length or gaudy color.

We use many kinds of spurs. Spurs, like any aid, vary in intensity; the desired intensity is determined by the horse one is riding and/or the job to be done. In this country we generally start with a short, dull Prince of Wales spur. Any less than that is what is called a "dummy spur," a spur with a neck so short as to be almost negligible. This might be a good spur for a touchy, hot, and extremely thin-skinned horse that never stops at a fence. Usually with sport horses, we are looking for a spur that produces more impulsion, especially now that we are dealing with more warmbloods and half-breds. Depending on the horse's responsiveness, the progression in intensity would be as follows: a longer Prince of Wales, a hammerhead, a dime rowel, a pointed rowel, a pointed German spur. Of course, there are other forms and variations, but these are the most common.

Once the rider's position and use of the aids have been established during flat work, and the right tack and equipment are in place, the style is pretty much set. All that now needs to be done is to coordinate this foundation with work over fences: namely, gymnastics at home and courses at horse shows. A rider's position and style and the horse's training are determined at home. It is too late to do so at a competition. Yes, horse shows are for learning, training, and improvement, but the real reason we go to horse shows is to win!

Chapter 7

The Rider's Technique
over Fences

Jumping Position
and Balance

To understand the American Jumping Style, one must know something about position over fences. Probably more than any other people in the world, Americans are concerned about position: not only because it looks good (esthetics are important to Americans), but also because form and position affect function and, of course, balance.

Position for jumping starts with the correct stirrup length. Correct stirrup length is essential for functional position and good balance over fences. While riding too short has its disadvantages, trying to jump with too long a stirrup is disastrous. This robs the rider of a correctly positioned lower leg and base, causes incorrect angles at the ankle, knee, and hip joint, and can lead to an insecure rider who cannot ride easily with the horse's motion. To check the stirrup length, the rider should stretch his legs down and see where the stirrup iron touches his leg. For dressage, the iron should touch the boot slightly below the ankle bone—while a good length for flat work, this is too long for jumping. For flat work, slow galloping, and low jumping, the stirrup iron should reach just to the bottom of the ankle bone; for jumping bigger fences, the top of the ankle bone; and for fast galloping and jumping very big fences, just above the ankle bone. Once the stirrups have been adjusted for jumping low schooling fences, a good rule of thumb is to shorten the leathers one complete hole (not a half hole) for every foot higher you plan to jump. (Another of Bill Steinkraus's excellent suggestions is to ride with longer stirrups the day after jumping so that one doesn't become accustomed to too short stirrup lengths.)

Just as in riding on the flat, placing the foot correctly in the iron is the next step. The stirrup iron should be perpendicular to the side of the horse, not to the rider's foot. Hence, the outside branch of the iron will be ahead of the inside, and the stirrup tread will cross the rider's foot at an angle. The ball of the foot rests on the iron, with the rider's little toe touching the outside branch of the iron. This foot-stirrup placement provides two things: enough security and support, and a very flexible ankle. Both are extremely important.

It is impossible to ride with an educated leg (and American jumping riders are famous for their legs) without the stirrup being on the ball of the foot. Once the foot is properly placed, the rider should relax the knees so that his weight can sink down into the heels. There must be sufficient weight in the heels for them to be driven down. Also, relaxing the knee allows the contact (grip) to go down into the calf of the leg and lets the toes come out a shade. The toes need not be forced out. They will go out just enough automatically when the knees loosen their grip. Forcing the toes in is a terrible sin—it brings the lower leg (the calf) away from the horse's side, and therefore it diminishes security and communication. It also locks the ankle, which then prevents the heel from sinking down sufficiently. In short, the position for the rider's leg when jumping is as follows: stirrup iron on the ball of the foot; legs under the rider with stirrup leathers perpendicular to the ground; knees relaxed, and contact between rider and horse distributed between the thigh, inner knee bone, and calf of the leg; heels down, ankles flexed, and toes out at a natural angle in accordance with the rider's conformation.

Working on up to the base of support—the thighs and seat—we find that this part of the rider's anatomy should be relaxed and, most of the time, deep in the saddle in three-point contact. Otherwise, when posting the trot, when galloping on straight lines, and during the flight of the jump, one is slightly out of the saddle in two-point contact. An educated horseman always exercises himself and his horse in both of these positions, or seats. When one rides exclusively in three-point contact, sitting in the saddle, he rides behind the motion at least part of the time. If he spends most of his time standing up in two-point contact, he will ride ahead of the motion. A combination of the two is best. Three-point contact gives strength and control; two-point contact gives balance and lightness, and it relieves the horse's back.

For galloping and jumping purposes, the basic position of the upper body is angled forward from the hip joint, approximately thirty degrees in front of the vertical. The rider's hip angle closes to assume this position, his back remains relaxed yet flat, and most important, his eyes stay up. This forward position is by far the most efficient for the horse as well as the rider. It is easier on the horse's back and puts the rider "with" his horse, not behind him. The jump is really an extension of the gallop—in fact, it is just another big galloping stride—so the rider in good position has little to do to catch up to the horse's jump. He is already there! Often though, especially at bigger, trappier fences, we must get "behind the motion" of the horse during the approach. The reason for this is to have more control and strength. In this case, the rider's hip angle opens, his upper body is closer to the vertical (or occasionally even behind the vertical), and his seat deepens toward the back of the saddle. His head and eyes must remain up.

A critical (and often neglected) part of the rider's anatomy for jumping work is his hands and arms. They are always crucial in riding, but I'd say especially so for galloping and jumping, where the horse's movements are so ample and elastic. The hands and arms must also be free and elastic, never fixed or rigid. Stiffness not only destroys the rider's feel and communication with his mount, but also ruins the horse's chances for any athletic endeavor of his own, such as galloping and jumping with a round bascule. A straight line from the rider's elbow to the horse's mouth encourages a light, elastic hand and arm. The thumbs are several inches apart, just inside the vertical, with the hands over and just in front of the withers. The most important thing about hands is that they be completely independent, relying on neither the horse's mouth nor the neck for support. One must *never* use the horse's mouth for balance or security. The hand must be completely free and independent to "take the mouth" and "give to the mouth."

Use of the Eyes in Jumping

Again, the use of the eyes is especially important for galloping and jumping. Things happen so quickly! The eyes must be up and ahead of the movement, as with driving a car on the highway, and fixed on a focal point aligned with the center of the fence or the rider's intended line. The eyes give the rider many things—for example, balance, direction, and coordination of the aids. When the eyes are up, these things are there; if the eyes drop, balance, security, and coordination fall apart.

With regard to direction, the eyes obviously show us the way. I never tell a pupil to lean in the direction he wishes to go (or, for that matter, away from the direction of movement). Instead, I simply tell him to "look," and his weight displacement will be automatic and perfect. The eyes control the rider's weight laterally, not so much longitudinally. The quickest way to get into trouble on a horse when jumping, or to have a runout or refusal, is to look down. Focus on your next fence and your horse will go there; look ahead over it, and the chances are that he'll go over it. I spend a lot of time practicing eye control exercises with my students, both on the flat and over fences.

Use of Hands in Jumping: Types of Releases

Probably the single most distinctive trait of the American Jumping Style is the use of the rider's hands during the jump—the *release*. The release permits the horse to use himself—particularly to extend his head and neck—without fear of being jabbed in the mouth or otherwise interfered with. Our horses use themselves well and jump with a beautiful bascule because we place so much emphasis on using our hands and arms in a classical manner—a manner so essential with the sensitive, athletic Thoroughbred horses we have grown up with. The release also requires the security and balance of a correct and classical jumping position.

Actually, a good rider should be able to execute several different releases and uses of the hand while jumping: the *long crest release* (with or without holding the mane); the *short crest release*; the *automatic release* (or "jumping out of hand"); various actions of the hand such as a rotation (or lift); and the opening, bearing, direct, and indirect rein aids.

The *crest release* is used primarily for beginner and intermediate riders, although it is also a valid and popular technique for advanced riders as well. Advanced riders often use the crest release when schooling very green horses over fences. In hunter classes, a long crest release can be a form of showmanship—a way of demonstrating to the judge that one's horse "goes on his own"—as well as a method of encouraging the horse to use himself well.

The first release that should be taught to every beginning jumping rider (and also to experienced jumping riders who have never learned basics) is the *long crest release with mane*. The rider's hands and arms reach halfway up the crest, press down, and pinch the mane between the thumbs and the first fingers. (If no mane is available because the horse's mane has been roached, a neck-strap can be used.) The beginning rider should execute the long release with mane three to five strides in front of the jump, and he should keep hold of the mane for a stride or two upon landing to *make sure* he doesn't come back on the horse's mouth or fall back in the air—the two cardinal sins!

When the rider places his hands halfway up the crest of the neck, his upper body is put into position—that is, forward and "with" the motion of his horse. If not put into this forward position, the beginner will surely be left behind. Holding the mane gives added security for the rider and is an "insurance policy" for the horse's mouth. The horse won't be hit in the mouth, and he has complete use of his head and neck. The disadvantage of this release is that the rider must surrender some control while his hands are placed on the horse's crest. However, a beginning jumping rider should not be learning to jump on a horse that requires constant contact!

The *short release with mane*, a few inches up the crest of the neck, should only be taught when the rider's hands automatically move up to the long crest release position at every jump. The short crest release still brings the upper body forward and still permits the horse's head and neck a certain amount of freedom, but it affords more control, which is its main advantage.

Intermediate riders have more security in their legs, heels, and base of support than beginners. They are ready to abandon the mane (which is really a crutch, but a good crutch) and learn the long release without mane, or *long crest release*. To perform this release correctly, the rider moves his hands halfway up the neck, rests his hands on top of the crest, and presses the weight of his upper body down into his hands. Like the long release with mane, this position gives the rider upper body support and helps his security while stabilizing his hands for the sake of the horse's mouth. Resting and pressing the hands on the crest is admittedly also a crutch, but to a lesser degree than grabbing the mane. In addition, pressing the hands forward and down against the crest helps to train the hands and arms to follow the motion made by the horse as he jumps. If the crest release is not executed correctly and the rider's hands float somewhere above the crest of the neck, the whole value of the technique is lost—it does not provide security, and it does not give freedom to the horse.

The long release provides maximum freedom for the horse and hence is useful over oxers, over gymnastics, and whenever the horse needs freedom to make a generous gesture with his head and neck. As the rider progresses past the beginner stage, he will be able to execute the long release as the horse takes off, instead of several strides before the jump. Technically, every rider, whether a beginner or an Olympian, should master this technique.

The *short crest release*, executed without the use of mane, is simply a modification of the long release. Where the long release ensures maximum freedom for the horse and the least risk of interference by the rider, the short release gives more control. To execute a short release, the hands move only a couple of inches up the crest of the neck from their normal position just above and in front of the withers.

They rest and press as in the long release. While freedom for the horse is a bit curtailed (but never to the point of interference), control is greatly enhanced. This release is often used when the rider must turn or balance the horse immediately after a fence. It is normally executed at the takeoff, rather than several strides before the fence.

Only intermediate and advanced jumping riders should use the short release, because beginners have neither the security, balance, nor timing to attempt it. They will only "stiff" the horse and restrict his use of his neck—or, worse, they will get "left behind"! Good intermediate or advanced riders should be able to use the long and short releases, with or without mane, according to the needs of the situation.

For elementary and intermediate riders to neglect the crest release, both long and short, is serious indeed. At this stage of riding, it is easy to get "left behind," the cardinal sin when jumping. Even if a beginner is athletic and precocious and manages to get by without going through the stages of the long and short crest release, he will most likely pay the price with his upper body. In compensating for what his hands are *not* doing, he will learn to duck over his fences, jump ahead, or drop back—or all of these bad habits may crop up!

The *automatic release* (also called "jumping out of hand") is for advanced riders only. An advanced rider over fences is one whose security, position, balance, and timing are absolutely solid. This technique requires perfect balance, coordination, and timing. It should never, never be attempted by a beginner or even an intermediate jumping rider. A mistake in timing, getting left behind, or jumping ahead of his horse should be a rare occurrence indeed for the truly advanced rider.

The rider gallops toward the fence, maintaining contact with his horse's mouth with a straight line from elbow to bit, with his hands slightly over and in front of the withers. As the horse takes off, he maintains this straight line and his light contact with the horse's mouth. Actually, if he does *nothing* with his hands (and if he has previously perfected his short release!), the horse will take his hands through the air, causing him to follow his horse's mouth with a light contact. Usually, when people *try* to follow the horse's mouth, they exaggerate and do it wrong. This advanced release is difficult because the rider must remain passive, doing "nothing" with his hands. Maintaining the straight line from elbow to mouth is important, as this allows the lightest, most elastic contact with the horse's mouth. When done well by an artist on horseback, it is a beautiful technique to watch. What's more, maximum control combined with sufficient freedom is the result. The goal of every advanced rider should be to jump with this automatic release, where the hands maintain a classical straight line from elbow to mouth and never need the support of the horse's neck. Very few people worldwide can use this release consistently well nowadays. Unfortunately, it is a dying art.

What is wrong today is that when riders reach an advanced level and are ready for the automatic release, they are not being taught it. A rider who is out of limit equitation classes and headed for Medal, Maclay, and USET classes should learn how to jump out of hand. The long crest release, while not wrong, is not what a judge should look for at this stage of riding. If he has two riders who are nearly equal, he should pin the one who is able to jump out of hand—a technique which shows better balance, security, and coordination. The crest release has gone overboard in this country today. It has become a mannerism, people can't live without it, and it is too often done wrong!

There has been much misunderstanding about the crest release, both in North America and elsewhere. I have always taught releases in this sequence: long and short crest release with mane, long (crest) release without mane, short (crest) release without mane, and automatic release. A rider should be able to execute the first three correctly before moving on to the automatic release, which is the ultimate goal. I do not believe in allowing beginners or even intermediate riders to attempt to "follow" the horse with an automatic release from the beginning; the poor horse will pay in the mouth for every mistake! However, many American riders, especially those in the equitation ranks, have unfortunately gotten sidetracked with the crest release, mistakenly treating it as an end in itself instead of a stage on the way to the automatic release. This has made the beautiful automatic release, once the norm for advanced jumping riders, something of a lost art. This is deplorable! The crest release is not and never was intended to be the be-all and end-all of jumping—it is a technique that, like any other, can be great when correctly used and no good if abused.

In order to work, any release must be executed correctly. When one is learning, teaching, or practicing the long or short release, with or without mane, details matter! If the hands are not placed at the right spot (halfway up the neck for the long release, a couple of inches up the neck for a short release), or if the rider "floats" his hands above the crest instead of pressing them firmly on top of the neck, neither the rider nor the horse gets the benefits of a correctly executed release. A "fake" release benefits no one! The hands should be side by side, not one in front of the other, and they should not be dropped down low alongside the horse's neck. Open fingers can let the reins slip and lose control; what's worse, the fingers may be sprained or broken.

Incorrect Use of the Hands and Faulty Releases

Faulty releases include the following: rotating the hands; throwing the hands; dropped release; and setting the hands. There are variations of these faults, but most fall into one or another of these categories. (Oddly enough, while these faulty releases produce poor results when used by elementary or intermediate riders, or when used excessively, most of them can occasionally be valuable when used by an advanced rider at the right time and place.) For instance, hands that *rotate* forward, upward, backward, or down are a serious fault that can interfere with the horse's mouth. These hands break the straight line from elbow to bit, and they result in a stiff, inelastic contact with the mouth. However, when done by an expert with perfect timing, such hands help to lift a horse off his forehand and can, on occasion, actually save a rail. All the good riders know this technique. However, it can get horses jumping hollow and stiff and is definitely not a technique to use too much. Horses learn to depend on the hand like a crutch.

Throwing the hands quickly forward is never good. This surprises a horse too much and can make a hot, quick horse quicker. If done at the wrong time, just *before* takeoff, it can amount to unexpectedly "dropping" the horse and can cause a bad mistake or even a stop. The technique is also rough and ugly-looking. Hands that are thrown forward often pick up the contact again just as abruptly. On the other hand, "throwing the horse away" in a slow, soft, and smooth way has great merit at times. For instance, to encourage a horse to think for himself, or, when schooling, to get a rub at a fence, this technique is not only valid but even classical. All the good riders today use this long release or smoothly "drop" their horses to get them jumping better in front, rounding their backs, and using their hocks.

A *dropped release* is one in which the hands drop below the horse's mouth. The rider's elbow angle is too open, which breaks the line from elbow to mouth downward and can restrict the horse's use of his head, neck, and front end. It also puts pressure downward against the sensitive bars of the mouth. While breaking the straight line upward is sometimes permissible, breaking the line downward is anything but classical.

Setting the hands downward against the neck instead of pressing forward into the crest has few advantages, save possibly serving as an emergency control "in the air." Setting the hands generally will intimidate the horse and make him jump flat and stiff. On rare occasions, I use this technique deliberately to stop a quick, strong horse in the air over a low fence, but to do so over bigger fences is most unfair to the horse and can cause an accident.

Seeing Distances

Seeing distances is something you feel, something intangible. Some people are born with an "eye for a distance." Yes, people can develop and improve their "eye," but there is no substitute for the natural jumping rider. People without the inborn sense of timing for a jump never become really good. They have no sense of stride and never get one.

The American Jumping Style is known for riders who look attractive, ride actively, and jump out of stride. Due to our hunter beginnings, we tend to jump from a longer stride than most Europeans, which isn't always the best for our horses' trajectory and bascule. Nowadays Americans more often look for a deeper distance, and more Europeans gallop and jump from a more even pace. The universal "eye" is becoming more standardized.

Sensing or seeing a fence is so simple that people complicate it, think about it too much, and consequently ruin it. One is galloping to a fence—any fence; he senses or sees a good stride and moves up to ask his horse. On the other hand, he senses that the distance is too long;

he waits, and there appears another, more comfortable distance. When one comes to a half stride, or in-between stride, a quick decision has to be made: leave out a stride or add one. If one could generalize, I'd say leave it out at speed or in jump-offs, but add a stride when going slowly.

The hands and arms are very closely connected with the rider's "eye." Why is that? Because the hands and arms are connected with the horse's mouth, and they move backward and forward, or oscillate, with the horse's mouth, neck, back, and stride. Hands that are tight and stiff make the rider's "eye" tight and stiff. If the arms are too loose, the "eye" will be too long and sloppy. One way to improve and/or change a rider's "eye" is to control and change his hands and arms. Shortening or lengthening the reins, holding the horse more or less— these are little things that can quite dramatically affect a rider's eye.

Chapter 8

~

Gymnastic Jumping:
Cavalletti and Beyond

~

There is probably no country, school, or style in the world that does not incorporate cavalletti and gymnastic jumping into the education of the horse and rider from the very beginning. Although use of cavalletti and gymnastic jumping originated with European trainers long ago, Americans have learned to apply this training in their own way, with a different emphasis. Perhaps the most important idea the American School has given the jumping world in recent years is this: the horse must be allowed to carry himself and do the work. This, in classical terms, is called self-carriage. When riding in the old-fashioned way, even over cavalletti and gymnastics, the rider felt obliged to "ride" the horse too much—helping, supporting, and dictating to it, and often doing more work than the horse. In the long run, this is not the best way to make a horse sharp, clever, or self-sufficient for the competition to come. Instead, it can make the horse depend too much on his rider to balance him, place him, and think for him; it can also distract some horses from the business at hand and engender resistance.

What Bertalan de Némethy did for American riders forty years ago was to emphasize and refine cavalletti and gymnastic training and to give us a system. His work with jumpers, coupled with the American professional's schooling methods for hunters, redefined the way we ride and school jumping horses. We learned to ride a relatively free horse over a series of closely related fences, teaching the horse not only to listen to his rider, but to balance himself, use himself athletically, and think for himself. We also learned to set up appropriate cavalletti and gymnastic exercises, to pay attention to how we approach them, and to stay out of the horse's way, allowing him to learn from experience.

In schooling gymnastics, lines, natural obstacles, and show jumping courses as a whole, the American ideology essentially concerns itself with two things. First, the horse (presumably having been well schooled on the flat) must really listen to the rider. The horse should remain as obedient, soft, supple, and relaxed as possible while responding to the rider's every demand. Second, the horse, being in this relaxed and rideable state, concentrates totally on the fence to be jumped. Only through such relaxed concentration can a horse and rider jump really well. Cavalletti and gymnastics, along with good flat work and a classic, functional position, are the means by which we accomplish this.

For cavalletti work and gymnastic jumping, American riders want their horses to approach the exercise in a slow but impulsive trot or canter. They do not override the horse; instead, they allow the spacing of the cavalletti or the distances in a gymnastic exercise to teach the horse to keep his own balance and learn from the exercise. The long release is often used, and the rider stays off the horse's back, allowing the horse to develop a good bascule and jumping style.

In schooling over gymnastics, every element and every inch of distance has its purpose. As the training progresses, both horse and rider become more experienced and more knowledgeable about the problems to be solved, and about how best to work together while solving them. Eventually, horse and rider are united; they become one. That is the beauty of really skilled riding and training.

The rider, during all his work over cavalletti and gymnastic jumping lines, concentrates in the same way that he does on the flat. He must influence his horse to go forward, come back, go straight, or turn left or right. His control must be as smooth and unobtrusive as possible ("invisible aids" again!) in order not to distract the horse from *his* primary job, which is jumping. The more excess motion on the rider's part, the more disturbing he is to the horse, both physically and mentally, and the consequences are likely to show up in jumping faults.

As the rider approaches a cavalletti or jumping exercise, his primary focus is on keeping his horse straight over the middle of the poles and maintaining a perfectly even pace. Since each horse's length of stride, temperament, and responsiveness are unique, the rider will quickly have to recognize the differences and adjust himself accordingly, so that he can adjust his horse.

Some horses have a normal length of stride but are a bit lazy. They must be animated by the rider's driving aids, but they must not be allowed to go faster or to run through the rider's hands. Other horses tend to move with shorter strides and a quick rhythm. They need to be slowed down and relaxed until their strides become quieter, longer, and even a little bit lazy. Still other horses may move with a very long but sluggish stride, leaning on the forehand. They will need to be animated by the rider's legs but held back by the rider's hands at the same time. The problems a horse displays over cavalletti poles in the very beginning will be a preview of what is to come over fences; a horse that is lazy, tense, quick, or poorly balanced over a single pole will show the same problems magnified over a larger jump.

There are several types of cavalletti and fences to be used in gymnastic work. Each has its own characteristics and purpose and tends to teach the horse specific jumping skills. By varying the types of cavalletti and obstacles as well as the distances, we can create a range of exercises that can be tailored to the needs and capabilities of any horse and rider.

A cavalletti (a single rail on the ground) is the smallest possible obstacle—a jump only a few inches high. Many fundamentals can be taught to the rider over this rail: position of the rider; use of eyes, hands, legs, and weight; upper body control; angles and turns; timing and seeing distances. Cavalletti are also very useful in training the horse in calm, forward, and straight approaches; regulating the stride; maintaining balance and rhythm; jumping in form with a good bascule; and correcting jumping problems.

The classical use of the cavalletti, as used by Bertalan de Némethy, one of the architects of the American Jumping Style, begins with a grid or series of three to six cavalletti, to be ridden at the trot. The spacing for the average horse is from four feet six inches to four feet nine inches. Cavalletti may be used on a circle or a serpentine; for canter work (spaced for a canter stride of twelve feet); as an element of gymnastic jumping lines; or in conjunction with a single fence.

One advantage of cavalletti is that they are so low that nobody can get into much trouble. A problem that surfaces over cavalletti can be solved without the more severe consequences that would occur if it happened over a much larger fence. This preserves the horse's (and the rider's) confidence. Another advantage is that cavalletti and low jumps can be jumped many more times without harm to the horse's legs. Meticulous horsemen like Bertalan de Némethy insist on a very stable performance over poles on the ground before going on to even a low cross rail. Only when the horse goes straight (without bulging to the left or right), maintains his rhythm, and neither rushes nor hesitates does the rider progress to the next step.

There are occasional exceptions. Some horses just do not like trotting over cavalletti, and no matter who is training these horses or how long they practice, they never really get good at it. Frequently the hot, sensitive blood horse that jumps well doesn't trot poles very well. Often this kind of horse is a careful jumper who would rather canter and jump over the poles than trot over them and perhaps stub his toe. In a way, this can be a "good" fault; it shows that the horse is just trying to jump high and clean.

Sinjon, my wonderful Olympic horse for the 1960 Rome Olympic Games, could jump any gymnastic, fence, or course like a cat. He was careful, fast, and very brave, and he had Olympic scope. The one thing he never did well was trot cavalletti. Even with the maestro himself, Bert de Némethy, he would hop, skip, and canter over the poles on the ground. Sinjon had a short, tense, irregular trot, and it was difficult for him to figure out the cavalletti. My best advice with horses like this is to compromise. Don't force the issue past a certain point, especially if the horse jumps the fences so well—that is what's really important.

Cavalletti should teach a horse to pick up his feet, and to be aware of where he puts his feet, right from the start. This is why solid cavalletti, built on fixed bases about four to six inches high, are the best. The horse should learn as early as possible that it stings a bit to hit a fence, and that being careless can cause him to trip or stumble. Sloppy jumpers are a disappointment at best; at worst, they can be dangerous.

The American Jumping Style is based on correct techniques. These techniques can never be learned by going fast or jumping big fences before the fundamentals have been established, because the rider cannot concentrate on his own form and on jumping a big fence at the same time. (The same can be said for the horse, too!) Exercises practiced over a pole on the ground or a series of cavalletti are ideally suited to teaching people to ride with sound basics and with style. The rider can concentrate on the exercise, because the cavalletti or "jumps" are very simple. Later, when the exercise has done its work and the correct technique is established as a habit, it will be second nature to the rider when he jumps larger fences. All of the fundamental techniques used in jumping are taught and confirmed over ground poles or cavalletti long before the thrill of that first "real jump."

Jumping Fences

If ground poles and cavalletti are step one for the jumping horse and rider, the cross rail is step two. In fact, for many years, the cross rail was a more common fundamental for Americans than the cavalletti. The cross rail is the most basic jump of all. It is used more than any other type of jump; because it is low and because of its construction, it invites horse and rider to jump the center of the fence. Because of their low height, cross rails cause little or no tension or excitement in either horse or rider. When a cross rail is placed at a measured distance (usually about ten feet) from the last cavalletti, it becomes easy for the horse to make a good approach and jump from the correct takeoff spot. All the rider has to do is keep the horse straight and maintain his rhythm and balance.

Step three, for developing both horses and riders, is a low, straight rail or vertical fence. The vertical teaches horses and riders to jump up, but not out. The horse must learn to use his forehand—his head, neck, shoulders, forearms, knees, and legs below the knees, all the way to the tips of his toes. Verticals also teach horses to use their back and hindquarters, study their fences, back off, and set themselves. This is very important to encourage clean, safe jumping.

When schooling over verticals, the rider must concentrate on keeping his horse straight and in the center of the fence. If he lets his horse drift to one side, there is no longer any need for the horse to jump squarely and in good form, with his forelegs folded evenly and tightly. He may learn to twist over his fences, "lay over" to one side, or hang a knee.

For the rider, jumping verticals develops precision, accuracy, and the ability to jump fences cleanly. Form and technique are the emphasis here, instead of the scope required by spread fences. Because there has traditionally been more emphasis on vertical fences than on spreads in our hunter divisions, many American riders feel more at home over vertical fences than they do over massive spreads, water, ditches, or banks. (This is a generality, and it is not as true today as it was twenty or thirty years ago.)

Spread fences test the horse's range or "scope"—his ability to jump wide as well as high. The easiest and most common type is the ascending spread, also called a "step oxer," constructed so that the back element is somewhat higher than the front. It is easy to jump because the lower front element gives the horse time to leave the ground and get his front end up before he encounters the higher back element. Even "hangers" (horses that hang their knees) can jump ascending spreads well.

Square oxers are as difficult to jump as step oxers (or ascending spreads) are easy. They are built with the front and back elements absolutely parallel and at the same height. The difficulty lies in the horse's need to get his front end up quickly over the high front rail, use his head, neck, and back to get across the spread, and kick up behind to avoid hitting either rail with his hind legs. The rider must take care not to override the first element (using too much leg), yet he still must use enough leg to get across the back rail. He must also avoid interfering with the horse's efforts to use his head, neck, and back, and must not come back prematurely and drop the horse's hind legs into the back rail. Most good trainers and course builders use square oxers a great deal; they teach horses a lot.

Swedish or cross rail oxers are popular today. Because the front and back elements are slanted in different directions, the lowest point of the whole fence is exactly in the center, but it is better strategy to jump the low side of the front element; this makes it a kind of ascending spread instead of a square oxer. The added factor in jumping this type of fence is line. Not only must the rider pay attention to pace and distance, but he must also be particular about the line he rides to and across the oxer. A steep Swedish oxer can appear formidable, and some horses may be intimidated and hang back, so the rider must be ready to give a very positive ride to these fences.

Also quite popular today is the narrow oxer, usually only a foot or two wide. These fences are used a lot nowadays for good reason— horses hit them if they don't keep their feet up. I find it works best to keep things simple and ride this skinny spread just like a vertical. It is important, though, for the rider to stay forward in the air and not to drop back too soon, because dropping back too early often causes a horse to hit this kind of fence behind.

Spread fences of more than two elements should also be included in schooling and gymnastic jumping. Probably the easiest type is the hog's back, which has a high middle element with a lower rail in front and behind. The shape of this fence conforms to the arc of the horse's jump and his bascule. The hog's back can be made more difficult by taking away the ground lines and by making the front and back elements higher and wider. This will penalize the extreme underride or override.

Triple bars are the most common form of three-element fence; they are a form of ascending spread, with each successive element higher. Like hog's backs, they are relatively easy to jump as a single fence. However, when used in combinations or related distances, or when going away from the in-gate, triple bars can ride long, wide, and flat. When set before a vertical, they can pose an especially difficult problem. I've always liked to use triple bars in my schooling at home. They teach riders a lot about impulsion and the art of driving a horse forward to and across a fence.

The fan is another variation of the triple bar, the difference being that one side is very high and the other is very wide. It is usually best to jump fans in the middle and avoid the extremes. A horizontal cross rail, where the rails are crossed in the air parallel to the ground (as opposed to a vertical, normal cross rail), can be psychologically tricky for both horse and rider, even though it is easy to jump if the line is accurately ridden and the rider is aggressive. I do use both of the foregoing fences at home from time to time, but never in gymnastics.

Ground Lines

Sophisticated trainers today make use of ground lines and elements to make their horses sharper and more clever, while educated course designers know how to use the look of an element or the placement of a ground line to create a "bogey" fence that is easy to misjudge.

Ground lines consist of elements that touch the ground, placed at the front, or takeoff, side of the fence. A simple ground line such as a rail or a brush box makes the fence easier to judge and to jump. If the ground line is colorful, unusual, or "spooky," it may draw the horse's attention to this part of the fence instead of the top rail, making him more apt to have a rail down.

A true ground line is placed just before or just under the first element of a fence; a false ground line is placed behind the front element. Some fences have no ground line at all. The easiest fence to jump has a ground line placed in front of the first element; next would come a ground line directly under the first element. A fence without a ground line is more difficult, and a false ground line (placed behind the front element) is the most difficult of all. Not only does a false ground line not encourage the horse to leave the ground soon enough, but it also can distract him from noticing the top rail of the fence. Fences without ground lines require concentration and can be educational, but only experienced or exceptionally clever horses can be expected to jump false ground lines without major problems. I start at an early stage to familiarize my horses with a wide assortment of fences with true ground lines, no ground lines, and occasionally false ground lines.

Natural Obstacles

Natural obstacles include hedges, dry ditches, water ditches, Liverpools, sunken roads (or grobs), banks of all kinds, and water jumps. These fences are important for teaching boldness, a "go forward" attitude, and the ability to cope with variety. Both horses and riders should become familiar and comfortable with natural obstacles from the beginning, so that these obstacles do not become something too special psychologically and a "big deal." They should be jumped singly at first and then incorporated into lines and combinations. The only reason we sometimes have a weakness over these fences when abroad is for want of practice over them at our shows at home. In Europe, these "funnies" (as they are called in England) are commonplace. Even experienced North American jumpers can be caught off guard and act a bit green over these jumps when they first jump in Europe. The remedies are to introduce such fences to *all* jumping horses and riders (including hunters and equitation mounts) at an early stage, and to include them more often in our competitions.

The single most important thing for both horse and rider to remember when tackling natural obstacles is *forward!* Galloping forward is a trademark of American equitation and the American Jumping Style. It is terribly important, when first introducing young horses to water, banks, ditches, and similar obstacles, to give them a powerful, positive override. Many a young horse is ruined forever by hesitating, missing the distance to a water, and having a fall. Since they are by nature not intelligent, but possessed of a great memory and trained by association, horses do not easily forget this bad experience.

Natural fences (banks, ditches, water, and the like) can also be incorporated into gymnastic jumping lines. This helps both horses and riders learn to handle them as normal, everyday obstacles, no matter how or where they encounter them. If natural obstacles are only jumped as single fences or on rare occasions, one can be undone when a ditch, bank, grob, or water is unexpectedly placed in a combination for a competition.

As a rule, however, gymnastic jumping exercises are conducted over fairly simple, "normal" vertical and spread fences. The unusual and more difficult fences are saved for special schools at home; often they only appear in special classes at horse shows. What is important is to master the height, width, airiness (lack of filling material), and distance problems between fences. It is also a good idea to use different-colored poles and to vary the appearance of elements such as walls, gates, and brush boxes. Eventually the horse must learn to accept jumps of any type or color and concentrate on the job of jumping the gymnastic.

Gymnastic Combinations

Once horse and rider have been introduced slowly and repeatedly to these low, single fences, it is time to put them together: first on a straight line, then on broken lines, and finally on curved or circular lines. Because the average jumping horse gallops with a twelve-foot stride, Americans have always used twelve feet as their standard measurement of striding, and these simple lines will be measured in increments of twelve feet. In the beginning, the fences will be spaced at generous distances of five strides or more; later on, the distances will be altered.

Combining fences in a line with closely related distances is called gymnastic jumping, because it affects the way the horse uses his balance and body when he jumps. The distances are extremely important; they can make a particular exercise easy, difficult, or even impossible for a certain horse. Gymnastics help a horse to discover and develop his own best jumping style; properly used, they can help him form the habit of using himself well when he jumps. Sometimes they can even help a bad jumper become a better one.

I had a young, green conformation hunter named Bonnie Castle who looked gorgeous but did not jump very well at all. (Conformation hunters are judged primarily on jumping style, although conformation and way of going also count.) As a first-year green hunter, even showing over fairly simple three-foot six-inch fences, he won very little. As a second-year horse, after a winter of cavalletti and gymnastics, he started jumping better and began to win quite a bit. By the time this horse reached the regular conformation hunter division, jumping four feet, he had "learned" through exercises to jump quite well; he was hard to beat. So that is a success story to give us all hope!

Combinations and "gymnastics" are really the same thing: a series of fences set close together. In competition, a combination never exceeds four fences in a row (except in the special six bars class). Schooling gymnastics, however, may have any number of obstacles. The problem posed by a combination or gymnastic is the rapidity with which a horse must go forward, come back, and go forward again. Combinations also require a rhythmic, athletic performance, not a desperate scramble. They are an "eyeful" to a horse. Some horses are more confident and comfortable jumping combinations than others, and certain horses are always somewhat overwhelmed by them. At the Grand Prix and Olympic level, it takes a lot of horse to negotiate a combination, no matter how well the rider rides. It can be said that it takes a good rider to jump big single fences, but it takes a good horse to jump combinations.

Combinations of two, three, or four elements may be composed of verticals, spreads, or both. Distances may be set for a no-stride (bounce), one stride, or two strides, and of course the required strides may be medium, short, or long. (A distance of more than thirty-nine feet is no longer considered a combination, but a "related distance.") Since verticals encourage the horse to get back on his hocks and jump "up," while spreads make a horse jump "up and out," the type of obstacles must be considered as well as the length and number of strides.

The shortest combination exercise is called a bounce or a no-stride combination. The horse must land and immediately take off again, without any intermediate strides. The average distance for a no-stride is twelve feet from one obstacle to the other, although the distance may vary from as little as eight feet to as much as fifteen feet. The exercise may incorporate a single bounce or a series of bounces or no-strides. The obstacles should be simple and not too high or too wide. Bounces teach horses to be clever and to think quickly; they encourage good use of the hocks and knees. They are also good for riders, improving their balance and athletic ability.

Here is an example of a simple gymnastic exercise incorporating no-stride combinations or bounces: three trot cavalletti, four feet six inches apart, followed by a distance of ten feet to a cross rail, followed by a distance of twelve feet to a straight rail, then another twelve-foot distance to a small oxer. This would be a series of no-strides or bounces. The horse should trot over the cavalletti and canter the rest of the gymnastic, landing and taking off from the same spot without putting in a stride between the obstacles.

Another example of a good gymnastic line would be as follows: three cavalletti, four feet nine inches apart, followed by an eleven-foot distance to a cross rail, a seventeen-foot distance to a small square oxer, a twenty-eight-foot distance to a small triple bar, and finally a forty-foot distance to a vertical. Here the horse should trot the cavalletti and the cross rail, then take one short stride to the oxer, two short strides to the triple bar, and three short strides to the last single rail. This gymnastic requires the horse to go forward over the spreads, but to come back and rebalance himself to deal with the short distances and the last vertical.

In gymnastic jumping, approximately 60 percent of the distances I set are short, 20 percent are normal distances, and 20 percent are long. The reason most distances are set short rather than normal or long is to teach collection to the horse. To shorten stride without losing sufficient impulsion is the most difficult challenge to ask of a horse, yet it is essential. Shortening the distance also forces the horse to use himself well when he jumps—he must jump off his hocks, push with his hindquarters, and use his head, neck, back, shoulders, and front end. He must jump round, "curling himself around the fence," instead of flat. Because we want the horse (and the rider) to learn to be clever and versatile—jumping out of a normal stride and off a long stride as well—some of the distances we set will be longer.

Related distances are fences close enough together to predetermine the number of strides from one fence to the next. As with combinations, the type of obstacles will have a bearing on the space available for strides, the optimum distance, and the way the fences should be jumped. The rider must be able to ride the right number of strides, either by "feel" or by counting strides. To achieve the best distance to the second fence, he will have to decide whether to shorten (adding strides), lengthen (leaving out a stride), or maintain the stride he has. On a broken line, bending line, or circular line (jumping on a turn), the added factor compounds the problem. The rider not only must control the horse's stride, but must accurately ride the track he has selected between fences. Permitting the horse to bulge outward or cut inward will alter the distance between related fences.

Most really good riders, whether on a hunter or a jumper, can predict their striding up to about nine or ten strides. Beyond that distance, I've found it simpler and less distracting to treat the striding as a "single fence" and ride it off my eye.

When measuring gymnastics, combinations, or related distances between fences, I've always found it best to work in multiples of twelve feet. If the distance is less than a multiple of twelve, the stride will be short; if a bit more than a multiple of twelve, the stride will be long. Of course, there will be situations in schooling, showing, and riding against the clock when a distance is on a half stride, just in between. Then it is the judgment of the moment or of that particular situation that determines whether one adds a stride or leaves one out.

It is easy to understand striding when beginning with a twenty-four-foot one-stride double, or "in and out." The normal jump out of a twelve-foot stride will cover twelve feet. The horse lands approximately six feet from the first element, takes one twelve-foot stride, and takes off six feet from the second element. To determine the number of strides in a given distance, divide by twelve and then subtract one twelve-foot stride (to allow for takeoff and landing). For instance, forty-eight feet divided by twelve is four, but after subtracting one twelve-foot distance for takeoff and landing, it would leave room for three twelve-foot strides.

Studying distances is an art unto itself, and every trainer must understand this fundamental to train any kind of jumping horse. The American Jumping Style has been developed over the years by practicing and solving almost every kind of distance problem imaginable. More than riders in any other country, we ride by knowing the distances and the number of strides between fences. (True, this can be carried to extremes—too many riders become obsessed with counting strides and use it as a crutch!) The distance factor between fences is critical to both horse and rider. Not only must the rider concentrate fully on whether to shorten, lengthen, or leave the horse alone, but he must also aid his horse in solving these problems between fences. By walking the course, the rider knows the problems beforehand; the horse doesn't.

There is no end to the possibilities of gymnastic jumping. Most modern trainers' jumping schools include some form of gymnastic. Combinations are part of every hunter and jumper course, and gymnastics are the only way to prepare horses and riders to jump combinations well. Gymnastic jumping is the quickest and best way to give both horse and rider the feel of what modern show jumping is all about.

One of the great American contributors to our use of gymnastics was Ben O'Meara, one of our most successful open jumper riders, horse dealers, and trainers until his tragic and untimely death in 1966. During the early 1960s he incorporated some wonderful exercises and ideas into his training of jumpers.

O'Meara would start with a cross rail (approached in a trot), followed by a series of square oxers about seventeen feet apart. There would usually be four oxers in all. After the horse had become accustomed to the exercise, he would eliminate the cross rail and just canter the multiple combination of oxers. These oxers were not small—they would be quite wide, five or five and a half feet. As the fences got bigger and wider, he would get more "generous" and space the fences about twenty feet apart.

Most of the horses O'Meara dealt with were hot Thoroughbreds off the race track; many had never jumped a fence before he acquired them. They got a "crash course" (literally and figuratively!) in doing this exercise daily. Because they were hot horses, they needed very little leg. O'Meara insisted on a long release (all his female jockeys could do it well!) and on using the opening or leading rein for steering. The cluck would more or less replace the leg aid. Through this system of riding, the horses had to learn to help themselves to the maximum. They were given minimum support from their riders, some of whom were fairly elementary themselves. (Kathy Kusner, later an Olympian, was the exception—she was O'Meara's star rider, with enormous talent and experience even at that point in her career.)

If a horse survived this training (and it was a hard test), he was quite a good horse. He had learned to fend for himself, to be quick in front and good behind, to get very round, and above all to concentrate on his fences. His scope and heart were stretched—these were big oxers! It was amazing that Ben O'Meara could produce jumper after jumper for the show ring in a matter of weeks. Even though they were still very green, they were bold, brave, and extremely careful, and they'd win. A long string of O'Meara's horses eventually jumped for the U.S. Equestrian Team, including the great Untouchable, Jacks or Better, and others.

Ben O'Meara's work must be touched on in any book on the American Jumping Style. He proved to be a major influence on our riding and training during the early sixties. While his ideas were not totally new (I'd been taught something similar by Gordon Wright,

Humberto Mariles Cortes, and Bertalan de Némethy), they were radically different to most American riders of that era, and they allowed both riders and horses to express themselves with a newfound freedom. Nowadays these ideas have leveled out and become less extreme; if Ben O'Meara had lived, I'm sure he would have, too. He was always ahead of his time. Just before he died, he showed and won at Hickstead; in fact, there is a big class named after him at the Hickstead show.

As a trainer, I do try to keep cavalletti and gymnastic work in perspective; I am not gymnastic-happy! I use them often, but only as a part of the horse's and rider's overall training, not to the exclusion of all else. All my horses and riders train over the same exercises. I don't build gymnastics to cater to a horse's good points or weaknesses. The only modifications I make would be the height and width of the fences, which in turn will modify the distance problem to some degree. Over time, a horse and/or rider that I train will face almost every kind of fence and distance problem.

Overtraining with gymnastics is certainly possible. In fact, most people tend to overjump their horses. They jump too high, too wide, and too much. Not only does this lead to horses physically breaking down, but they also get stale and bored and start jumping poorly. Overschooling any facet of a training program is a mistake. Horses don't learn best that way; they thrive on variety.

Some "chicken-hearted" jumpers (especially the kind that jump awkwardly and hang their legs) can be easily frightened by tight, airy gymnastics. So can horses with too long or too short a stride. A frightened jumper usually shows it by stopping, twisting, or hanging his knees. As a rule, the only concession I make is to keep the jumps low; I don't usually change the distances. Horses can and must learn to solve distance problems even at a very low height.

An exercise that I like, which can be incorporated into gymnas-

Jumping on a Circle   The American Jumping Style, coupled with a gymnastic approach to training jumpers (from the work of Bertalan de Némethy), has produced marvelous results for years. This interesting picture taken at Aachen shows me at the center of the circle. Eric Wauters (Belgium) has cantered the cavalletti (seen in the background) and is now negotiating a small vertical as he continues on a circle to the right. This exercise will relax and soften the horse, and it helps produce better turns in the ring.

Vertical, Cavalletti, Vertical   This "triple" combination gymnastic is designed to slow the horse down and teach him to concentrate on both his front and hind ends. The distance between each pair of elements is probably eleven to twelve feet. At this height, the chances are that the horse will lightly rub the jumps, which will sharpen him up. Alice Debany is showing the long release perfectly. She has rested both hands halfway up the horse's crest. This is a good moment to use this release. Notice her depth of heel and leg position.

The Approach (1)

We spend a great deal of time lowering the horse's head; when done properly, it is good for the horse both physically and mentally. However, as seen in this photo, horses often raise their heads when galloping and jumping. Here I have maintained a straight line from elbow to mouth by raising my hands. Also notice how my weight is distributed between my heels, crotch, and buttocks, with the upper body inclined forward, and the eyes focused up and ahead.

The Approach (2)

Just before the takeoff, the horse extends and lowers his head and neck and brings his hocks under him; all this enables him to lighten and free his shoulders. The rider's heels remain well down, his seat deepens into the back of the saddle, the upper body remains inclined forward "with the motion," the eyes are up, and the hands yield toward the horse's mouth. Once the distance has been established, balance, impulsion, support, and freedom are all important.

The Takeoff

The horse crouches like a cat. First he slams up off his shoulders; then he thrusts from his hocks. The rider here is well forward, being "with" his horse so his upper body weight does not interfere in any way. His hands now are light and low, maintaining the all-important line from elbow to mouth. His heels remain down and his eyes up.

The Flight (1)

The horse's shoulders and front legs rise; his head must be allowed to extend out and down. Because of the steepness of the flight, the rider's upper body stays very far forward so as not to interfere with the horse's back. The well-depressed heels provide maximum security for the rider. The eyes stay up; the back is flat; and the hands remain yielding and, if possible, in line with the horse's mouth.

The Flight (2)

The rider's style permits him to function, giving his horse the best ride and a fair chance. This big horse is showing us an impeccable style over this vertical. His knees are tight to his chest, and he is jumping "round" by extending his head and neck and using his back. The rider is displaying the American Jumping Style, from the turnout of horse and rider to the position of his lower leg. A leg that is fixed like this one does not irritate the horse by swinging back.

The Landing

As the horse lands, the shock of landing is absorbed in the horse's joints. It is the same with the rider. The shock absorbers are in the rider's ankles, which are flexed down and in; his knee angle closes as he sinks (not sits) into the saddle. The hip angle opens slightly as the rider straightens up a bit in order to use his weight. The hands come back into position, and the eyes remain focused on a point ahead.

The Departure

Galloping away from a fence, the rider assumes a two-point contact with just his two legs in contact with the horse and his seat slightly out of the saddle. This position makes it more comfortable and less tiring for both horse and rider in galloping work. The rider's heels remain well down, his back is flat, his eyes and head are up, and his hands maintain a perfectly straight line from elbow to mouth. The horse is in his natural frame and balance for the extended gallop.

The Approach—Classic Position   Joan Scharffenberger, on the approach a stride before takeoff, is perfectly positioned. Her stirrup is on the ball of her foot; her heels are down; her toes are out; her leg is back and on her horse. The base of support (thighs and seat) has dropped down and back into the saddle; it is deep. Her upper body is inclined forward about thirty degrees, with her eyes up. Her hands are moving forward in order to release her horse's mouth, and there is a straight line from elbow to mouth. Her horse's wonderful expression shows how he appreciates his rider's correct position.

The Takeoff—Classic Position   Scharffenberger's heels remain driven down, the leg neither too far forward nor too far back. Her seat is just about to be thrown forward and out of the saddle by the horse's thrust. Her eyes remain up as her hip angle closes, putting the upper body forward. Her hands move forward into the crest of the horse's neck. The alert concentration of the horse shows that he is not being distracted by his rider.

The Flight—Classic Position This picture is most exemplary of the current American Jumping Style. Isn't it remarkable how Scharffenberger has maintained a perfect leg position—it couldn't be better! Her hands, demonstrating a long crest release, are most correct for what is popular today, not only in America but around the world. The horse must like her position—he's giving this fence a foot to spare.

The Landing—Classic Position Scharffenberger, due to the placement of her stirrup on the ball of her foot and the weight in her heels, is beautifully demonstrating a flexible ankle and other "shock absorbers." Her seat sinks softly and slowly back into the saddle. Her hip angle opens, straightening her upper body, while the eyes stay up, focused on a point ahead. Her hands come back into position, resuming contact with the horse's mouth.

The French Style

Durand has pivoted on his knees a bit here, which swings his leg back too far. This is more of a European habit, both physically and mentally. The American Jumping Style stresses lower leg contact to such an extent that riders of that style rarely get into this habit. Nonetheless it is easy to see the proximity of the French and the American ways of riding.

Short Stirrups

Robert Smith is in a very classic position despite the fact that his stirrups are too short. Steinkraus, the all-time greatest exponent of the American Jumping Style, taught us always to lengthen our stirrups two to four holes the day after a horse show, thus ensuring that we would not develop the habit of riding too short. Riding too short will force the knees up and the buttocks back too far; you can clearly see it here.

Jumping Ahead

The only thing worse than too short a stirrup when jumping is too long a stirrup. Both extremes promote "jumping ahead." Here Smith's knee angle has straightened out too much, and his base of support (seat and thighs) is too far out ahead of the saddle. This is a most precarious position—if a horse puts in a short jump or stops, the rider can be popped off. However, the rest of Smith's position is really beautiful.

Landing—Shock Absorbers

It is most important to understand the concussion, or shock of landing, on a horse, be it at a trot, gallop, or jump. The rider absorbs shock through the major angles of the ankle, knee, and hip. Because Walter Gabalthuler of Switzerland has learned to control these angles correctly, he is able to land off a jump softly and, therefore, not irritate or distract his horse. The rider has learned through his American Jumping Style training that angle control and "soft" landings are all important.

Eyes   Gabalthuler displays perfect eye control, looking to the left in anticipation of a left turn. What is most important and instructional about this photo is that he is looking while still in the air, before landing. By doing so, he will make the turn smoothly and on time. Anticipation is so important in riding. Never be late on a horse!

Galloping Position   Mirri Kynsilhto of Finland has been trained extensively in the American Jumping Style and has thoroughly adopted this style to galloping between fences. Her stirrup is on the ball of her foot, although a trifle too far back here. The heel is down, and the stirrup leather is vertical. Her base of support is out of the saddle, displaying a two-point contact for galloping on straight lines. Her eyes and head are up, her back is flat, and her upper body is inclined forward approximately thirty degrees. There is a straight line from her elbow to the horse's mouth.

Approach—Three-Point Contact Katie Monahan-Prudent—not only one of the greatest riders of all time of either sex, but a great champion of the American Jumping Style—is approaching this fence in three-point contact: her seat and her two legs. This position is mandatory for jumping and for turning. The rest of her position is also very classic.

Takeoff—Two-Point Contact As the horse takes off, he thrusts Monahan-Prudent out of a three-point contact and into two-point contact. Only her legs are now in contact with the horse; her seat is no longer in the saddle. It is very important to understand these two positions and when to use each. The American Jumping Style is very particular about when one is "up," or out of the saddle, and when "down," in the saddle. The rider should be "down" about 80 percent of the time, and "up" only abut 20 percent.

The Approach—German Style

This is a classic three-point approach, no matter what rider or what country. Slootaak (Dutch-German) is in beautiful position: soft, balanced, and with his horse. If we were to get very particular, his back is a bit round and his leg a little too far forward. Notice how the horse is studying the fence, extending his head and neck and supporting himself on his shoulders.

Takeoff—German Style

Slootaak is very characteristic of the Dutch-German way of riding. His heels have come up at the takeoff, and his seat has jumped out and ahead of his saddle and his horse. This is partly due to the fact that he doesn't move his hands very much. Slootaak's seat and upper body are doing more work than his hands; the American Jumping Style teaches just the opposite. For the beginner or average rider, these form faults could spell disaster, but for Slootaak, a rider of genius, they don't much matter.

Uphill Gallop

Many horses like to raise their heads and necks when approaching a jump. The best thing to do is what Monahan-Prudent is doing— follow with the hands and maintain the line from mouth to elbow. It is never wise to contradict nature. This is a wonderful picture of galloping "uphill." The horse is in balance: his hocks are engaged, carrying the weight, while his shoulders are free and light. This position certainly beats galloping "downhill," with the horse's head low and all the weight on his shoulders.

Relaxed Concentration Slootaak and his horse clearly display the mental qualities needed for competition riding and jumping: relaxation, alertness, intelligence, and concentration. Yes, we do work hard on our own physical mechanism and on that of the horse. However, it is only when the physical is perfected that we can forget about it and set it free. Then we can work on the mind of horse and rider, which is what this sport is all about.

European Hand and Leg
This could never be an American rider—Slootaak's hand and leg are a giveaway. This very low "automatic" release with a broken line below the horse's mouth is rarely if ever seen in North America. While one does see riders pivoting on their knees all over the world, it is much less common in North America than in other countries.

The American Crest Release   Here Hap Hansen shows us perfectly how to place the hands for the long crest release. The hands are placed on and pressed into the crest of the horse's neck. A long release such as this is placed halfway up the horse's neck. A short crest release only moves an inch or two.

Fingers   The same rule holds true in jumping as in dressage: relax the hand but do not open the fingers (except in an emergency when you have to drop the reins). Not only are open fingers an unsightly habit, but one can lose the rein, the mouth, and the control, and easily break a finger!

Classic Example of a Pivoting Leg
By gripping excessively, the knees act as a pivot, and the legs will swing back. When the rider distributes the grip among the thigh, inner knee bone, and calf of the leg, the leg will stay in place. This distribution of contact with the heels down, toes out, and calf in contact with the horse's side is part of every American's riding education, but it is still foreign to many Europeans.

Loss of Leg While in the Air
Little good comes of the heels coming up and the lower leg leaving the side of the horse. The heels should act as an anchor, and the flexed ankle as a shock absorber; in other words, one's security in the saddle is provided by an educated lower leg. Once the lower leg is gone, as shown in this photo, then the rest of the rider's body—his base, upper body, hands and arms, and balance—is gone too.

Toes Down
I am a great believer in an educated and beautiful lower leg. American riders are known for their leg position. This European rider's leg position is outdated, though still far too common. He is pinching with his knees; his lower leg has slipped back and off his horse; his toes are down and his heels up. This faulty leg position has irritated his horse—notice the swishing tail.

A Too Short Running Martingale
Americans have always been wary of running martingales. They prefer standing martingales, and with good reason. A short running martingale, such as this one, bears down on the sensitive bars of the horse's mouth, causing him to raise his head against the pressure and, consequently, hollow his back. Thoroughbreds especially cannot tolerate this abuse and will have faults behind. While this rider's position is very correct, not only is the martingale excessively short, but so are the stirrups.

A Broken Line—
Below the Horse's Mouth
A straight line from the rider's elbow to the horse's mouth is always correct; so usually is a line broken upward, above the horse's mouth. Very rarely is a line broken downward below the mouth (here caused by too tight a running martingale) good at all. Here it is clearly seen how hitting the delicate bars of the horse's mouth raises his head, stiffens his back, and restricts his hind end.

Dropping Back in the Air
David Broome and I call this the "old man's disease" because most older riders tend to do it. Who knows why? It is probably a combination of physical and mental factors. Here I am coming back too early over the back rail of an oxer. Fortunately, Jane Clark's "Rio" had such a fabulous hind end that it rarely affected him (he almost never had faults behind).

Course Analysis

When it comes to strategy, one cannot overprepare. Here Kynsilhto and I discuss and analyze a course together. A good trainer must understand every stride, turn, and angle when helping riders understand a course. Nowadays, course analysis is fairly universal; riders and trainers from all over the world walk and understand a course quite the same.

The American Jumping Style

Tony D'Ambrosio is a perfect example of the style we have developed in this country. His toes are out, heels down, ankles flexed, calf in contact, base up out of the saddle, upper body forward, and arms in a straight line from elbow to mouth. He uses only a snaffle bridle, with no martingale at all. This photo exemplifies total control coupled with maximum freedom.

Just Before Takeoff

The heels remain down and in, the toes out, the ankles flexed, and the lower leg in contact with the horse. The rider's buttocks drop down and *back* into the saddle and the horse's back—relieving the horse's shoulders and weighting the hindquarters, and thus aiding the horse's balance. The upper body remains forward, up to but no more than thirty degrees in front of the vertical, with the eyes up. The arms and hands become lighter and softer, allowing the horse freedom to use his head and neck as a balancing agent. Nothing should hinder the head and neck during the last minute of the approach, the takeoff, the flight, or the landing.

During Flight

The rider's legs stay in place with the ball of the foot on the stirrup, the heels down, and the lower leg in steady contact with the horse. The rider's base of support (thighs and seat) is thrown out of the saddle by the horse's thrust—the rider doesn't "jump" himself ahead of the horse. The upper body is parallel to the horse, with the eyes up and focused ahead. The rider's hands are generous and giving in the release of the horse's mouth. D'Ambrosio is showing us a beautiful example not only of the American Jumping Style, but also of power, support, and sympathy—qualities that should mark every jumping rider.

Finishing the Course

It is never a good idea to jump the last fence and then pull up and drop the reins. D'Ambrosio is showing us how to school the gallop before retiring from the arena. What a beautiful example of the collected jumping gallop, not only in the rider's very classical position but also in that of the horse. Notice the engagement of the horse's hindquarters and the flexion of the horse's mouth. These give the "rounded" topline that is so necessary if we want suppleness and relaxation to be a part of our horse.

Michael Matz on the Approach

Again we see the classic American Jumping Style in action. The stirrup is on the ball of the foot (in this case, almost too near the toe), the heels down and in with the ankles flexed, the lower leg in contact, the buttocks weighting the back of the saddle, the upper body inclined forward about thirty degrees with the eyes up, and the hands and arms soft and pliable. Notice how the fingers are correctly around the reins, not open. Matz is definitely supporting a well-balanced horse just before takeoff, neither hindering nor abandoning the animal.

Matz Taking Off

The first thing that strikes me about this photo is how beautifully turned out both horse and rider are. *Everything* is perfectly clean. However, as a horseman, technician, and artist of the highest class, Matz is entitled to stray from perfect form. He does jump ahead of his horses a bit (notice how his seat and thighs are ahead of his saddle), and he does place his stirrup more on his toe than on the ball of his foot. Both of these habits would surely be serious faults in an average rider.

Matz During Flight

This is truly a beautiful jumping picture. Why? First, the horse is showing a near perfect bascule. He is so round, dropping his head and neck, using his back, and "jerking" his knees, all things we as horsemen appreciate. Second, the rider is impeccably turned out and in beautiful style. I particularly like his hands; they are alongside the horse's neck and in line with the horse's mouth.

Matz on Landing

The heels are well down, and the ankles are absorbing the shock of landing. The rider sinks down softly into the saddle only *after* the horse has cleared the obstacle with his hind legs. The hip angle opens, and the rider assumes a galloping position, maintaining a light contact with his horse's mouth; his eyes are up and ahead. Notice how much strain is placed on the horse's legs upon landing from a fence. For this reason, horses must be thoroughly legged up before jumping, and they should never, never be overjumped.

tics, is walking and trotting over low fences. This is good for horses because it teaches them to jump off their hocks, to use themselves well, and to wait and not rush their jumps. It also teaches riders to wait, not to anticipate their fences, and to quickly yet smoothly coordinate their aids. For walking and trotting, fences up to three feet are usually high enough. However, with talented riders on good jumping horses, trotting higher fences and even some spreads is an excellent exercise.

Jumping on angles, curves, turns, and roll-backs is good for every horse, especially for the jumper and the equitation mount. Fancy conformation hunters must be without blemish, so they are not usually subjected to sharp turns or exercises that might cause some lumps and bumps. However, all other jumping horses should be prepared for this type of problem. When I school angles and turns, I do not jump too high, too wide, or too fast. I do train the horse to turn very tight to the fence and immediately after the fence, as well as to turn in the air. Though some horses seem to take to these turns naturally, all horses must be taught and need to practice this technique.

As far as I'm concerned, the training for young horses, be it flat work or jumping, is all the same. Whether they are destined to end up as hunters, jumpers, or equitation horses doesn't matter; they all come up through the ranks the same way. They all do basic dressage, gymnastic work, colorful fences, and natural fences. I believe in developing all the essentials in a well-schooled, good jumping horse. Confidence, heart, form, scope, carefulness, cleverness, and rideability must all be instilled into the jumping equine athlete. If any of these factors are missing, the horse won't go very far.

What I emphasize and believe strongly in is a balance of repetition and variety. A horse has the mentality of a two-year-old child; that is not very bright! Horses do have good memories, and they learn by association. Like riders, horses will sometimes surprise you. Just by doing it over and over again, they can get it—even the not-so-talented ones. I put young or difficult horses into my regular, basic lesson program. Because I school my horses over all kinds of low but varied fences and exercises, they develop confidence and boldness. This is the rule of repetition and variety.

Chapter 9

~

Jumping Courses

~

Jumping courses successfully is the culmination of all the work, exercises, and maintenance done at home. If there is a stone left unturned in preparation, there will be a fence down in competition.

First, last, and foremost comes the care and management of the horse—his physical and mental well-being and comfort. How can a horse (or any athlete) go to a competition without feeling good in every respect? He can't! If his condition is not at peak, his legs not tight and sound, his feet shod incorrectly, and his brain not on the job, success will not be forthcoming. As caretakers of their horses, Americans are second to none. One of the strongest cornerstones of the American Jumping Style is stable management—the care of the horse and all the equipment that goes with him. Stable management (including veterinary care and shoeing) is the *sine qua non* of any kind of success with horses.

After care and stable management come flat work, longeing, handling, turning out, and, especially, good riding—all contribute to making the horse *rideable*. One can never have a horse too well "broke" for jumping.

As we've said, gymnastic jumping is the modern exercise approach to preparing horse and rider for jumping courses. This progressive system, which uses specific exercises to develop good habits and cure problems, has been used for years in other sports but is relatively new in the sport of riding. One rarely jumps a whole course at home, but rather lines, combinations, or parts of the whole. Normal turns found in courses and "time" turns used in speed events should also be well rehearsed at home before they are encountered in actual competition courses. One does not ride to win the competition at home, but rather on the playing field.

Some of the components I usually include in a schooling course at home are: a related distance on a straight line that can be jumped in both directions (vertical to spread and spread to vertical); two, three, or four fences on a broken line (a curved or bending line, or fences offset from each other) with related distances; a narrow, "skinny" fence (with rails only six to eight feet long); a Liverpool (indoors or outside); natural (outdoor) fences such as banks, ditches, water, and grobs; a triple bar and/or Swedish oxer; and at least one combination with two to four elements. I usually build fences wider rather than higher, and I make great use of true and false ground lines and fences without ground lines. I set very few "normal" distance problems at home; instead, they are a little long, a little short, or off stride—or they offer an option. I build courses both indoors and outdoors, and I frequently change the location, types, and appearances of the fences. I also incorporate different kinds of natural obstacles into most schooling courses.

Fortunately for all of us riders, teachers, and trainers, our course designers of today are universally building more intelligent and sophisticated courses. The days of going into overdrive and attacking the fences with big spurs and crude aids are over. Nowadays, relaxed obedience is the key to jumping courses well. *Preparation* is the key to having a horse capable of being ridden well over today's courses, and many a class is lost or won by what has—or hasn't—been done beforehand.

Once all the foundation blocks are in place, five factors must be put into effect to ride a course of fences successfully. Number one is *pace*. Establish the pace for that particular part of the course. Pace and stride are closely related. The faster one goes, the longer the horse's stride; the slower we go, the shorter the stride should be. In jumping courses, Americans tend to set the pace at a smooth hand gallop between fourteen and sixteen miles per hour before going to the first fence. It is easier to shorten or lengthen a stride from this medium pace than if one started out too slow or too fast.

The second factor in riding a course is *line*. There is a line to and after every fence. While the basic line is a straight line perpendicular to and over the center of the fence, there are also curved lines, broken lines, and angles. Especially when one is riding against the clock, the line to a fence is a critical factor. Riding a line must be second nature to a show jumping rider. He must know how to ride all the different kinds of lines, and he must choose the best line to each fence for the situation at hand.

Pace and line combine to bring us to the third factor: *distance*. The distance factor has to do with bringing the horse to the fence so that he takes off neither too long nor too short. Not only does the rider have to put the horse right to the fence, but he must also be able to put him a little long or a little short, depending on the horse and the problem at hand. Unfortunately, a "sense of distance" is not inborn in every rider (or every horse, for that matter!). Learning to sense distances can be done, if one really wants to devote a lifetime to jumping fences. However, in the end, nothing seems to beat a born "eye."

Balance is our fourth factor. A sense of balance is much like a sense of distance but is easier to acquire; there is no fence in the way!

When a horse is galloping on course, no matter how fast, his hocks should be under him and he should be "together." This is galloping equilibrium. If the horse loses this balance, his hocks are out behind him and he becomes "strung out." Some horses are difficult to keep together in balance even at a slow canter, while others are never out of balance no matter how fast they gallop. The same applies to a rider's sense of balance; some riders feel it, and other riders don't. Nevertheless, given time, a sense of balance can and must be acquired if horse and rider are to jump courses successfully.

Our last (but by no means least) factor is *impulsion*. Impulsion is energy, activity, liveliness, RPM's—but not speed! Speed does possess its own inherent, built-in impulsion, but speed and impulsion are not the same thing at all. To give an example, a piaffe or trot in place has tremendous impulsion at zero (or nearly zero) miles per hour, while a sloppy four-beat canter at twelve miles per hour has much less impulsion than the piaffe. A sense of impulsion is best acquired by horse and rider through training over gymnastics. In that way, both feel how much impulsion is required for jumping different types of fences off different strides—short, medium, and long. Even very gifted riders need to experience many different situations on many different horses in order to gain a real sense of impulsion.

While I've listed impulsion last among our five factors in jumping, it is certainly not the least. When I ride a horse, the first point I insist on is immediate obedience to my legs—that he go instantly forward. Impulsion is the first and last and most essential factor in all riding. Without correct impulsion, nothing else is really possible.

Walking the Course

Before jumping a modern, technical, sophisticated course, one must walk the course and analyze it. That is only fair to the horse. Things are too complex today to "wing it." As I walk a course, I follow the line I intend to ride—straight, curved, or broken. I note the distances by taking four three-foot strides for every twelve-foot gallop stride. Using my system of multiples of twelve feet, I will analyze the pace I want for each line, as well as where I will need to move up and where I must take back. These two factors (line and pace) should help me sense the right distance to each fence. Hopefully, in practice, my sense of balance and impulsion won't let me down. While walking the course, I will also walk and analyze the jump-off course, with special attention to the best lines, turns, and distances for riding against the clock.

When I walk a course at a show, I pay particular attention to where the start and finish lines are for both the first round and the jump-off. (I will not be able to walk this course again before the jump-off!) The start and finish lines not only will tell me where the course begins and ends, but may also show me how to save ground and time in lining up with the first fence and getting to the finish line after the last fence.

When walking a course, the rider must closely examine the construction of each fence and decide where and how to approach it, jump it, and land after it. I don't usually need to feel a fence or shake the rails to evaluate it. I can see which fences use lighter, flatter cups, and I figure that all fences will come down if rapped anyway.

Everybody today walks off the striding of related fences—that is, fences set less than ten (galloping) strides apart. If you train yourself to take a three-foot stride, four of your strides will equal one twelve-foot canter stride. From this basic measurement, it is easy to see if a distance is short, long, or normal. For distances of more than ten strides, I forget about walking off the number of strides; it's less confusing and easier to ride it off my eye. Sometimes people today make riding too mechanical —the number of strides is not a magic key to success.

A rider should pay particular attention to the turns when walking the course. Turns are time savers or time wasters in the initial round, and they are what win or lose classes in jump-offs and speed competitions. Often people get so wrapped up in walking the lines that they forget about planning how to ride the turns.

Under most circumstances, it is enough to walk the course once and then walk the jump-off course. Some people walk and think too much and only mix themselves up. Concentration is what is needed— not obsessive rewalking and worrying. However, for a major competition like a Grand Prix or a Nations Cup, I would advise walking both the first-round course and the jump-off course several times to get them absolutely clear.

Last but not least, before leaving the ring on foot, I plan my entrance circle. Without getting too close to any particular fence, I want to let my horse get a feel of the surroundings, go into a spooky corner of the ring, and pass by an unusual fence or a combination. This is not illegal and, cleverly done, can be most helpful. I often do the same thing when making my way to the exit after finishing a course, thus preparing the horse for the next class. This is only good, smart horsemanship.

Juniors and amateur riders are taught to mimic the professional riders in their course walk. There is one big psychological difference. Amateurs and juniors often have to be "pumped up" and made to develop an aggressive attitude for certain courses or classes; professionals are already aggressive. But against the clock, juniors and amateurs all around the world can go incredibly fast, sometimes faster than the pros. Sometimes ignorance is bliss!

The biggest and most unpredictable factors in jumping horses, both at home and in competition, are weather and footing. Often the most wonderfully prepared horses and riders go down the drain because of these factors, and it is often not their fault. Therefore, although it is sometimes a hard experience to bear, horses and riders alike need to experience competing in foul weather with deep or slippery footing. This toughens up human and equine athletes alike. Horses must be shod properly and equipped with the right kind of calks for different footing conditions. It is up to both the trainer and the rider to learn about shoeing and which calks to use when; this is one of the most crucial factors in competing with jumping horses. No matter how a horse is shod, never forget to override in the mud. Mud takes a lot of leg!

After a short warm-up over a few trotting fences, oxers, and verticals, I will enter the ring. Within the limits of the one-minute rule, I'll allow the horse to become familiar with the ring and even some of the spookier fences on the course. Of course, I never actually show a horse a fence; that is cause for elimination. Before the minute is up, after the bell has rung, I've established a smooth hand gallop and am crossing the starting line. It is always better, in the interest of impulsion as well as staying within the time allowed, to jump the first fence a little faster than you think you should. From there on, one follows the plan established by the course walk as closely as possible. Shorter turn here, wider turn there, angle this fence to set up a slight broken line, jump into this line a little stronger, or perhaps a little slower coming to that vertical in-and-out. The plan should be definite and set, but what sets the good rider apart from the mechanical rider is that he can improvise and cope within the plan if need be or if things go wrong. Especially for jump-offs and speed classes, one must have a definite, down-to-the-last-stride riding plan, but one must be able and willing to improvise when it becomes necessary. For every stride lost, one is a fraction of a second slower.

Even while completing the course and crossing the finish line, one should still be training the horse. To pull up and then drop the reins is bad discipline and sloppy horsemanship. Rather, finish by cantering a large circle, making sure that your horse is in front of your legs and yielding to your hands, just as you would in training at home. Then walk and lengthen the reins. I am also not a fan of feeding horses treats as they exit the arena with their bridles on. Horses are drawn to the in-gate like magnets already, so why make it worse by feeding them at the gate? Reward to a horse is a good ride, nothing more, nothing less. Certainly a lump of sugar or a handful of grass is no replacement for a good and fair ride.

Bad fences, bobbles, or disasters on course happen to everyone, even the very best. The answer is to quickly analyze what happened, but at the same time ride forward, toughen up, and become more aggressive. Unless it is really a wreck, the rider should not pull up or circle because of a mishap on course. That is the sure sign of a weak, "chicken-minded" rider. Once people start pulling up it becomes a habit, making them more and more tentative and often leading to worse trouble.

When a rider misses a distance on course or has a bad fence, he must pull himself together and get positive with his eye. If a horse hesitates or "chips in" at a jump, lay a stick on him at the next fence, get him listening to the leg, and put the heart back in him. On the other hand, if a horse rushes and runs past the distance and through a fence, it is best to hold him together, go slow, and make him shorten up and add strides to the next couple of fences. While a horse cannot be behind the rider's leg, he cannot be in front of the rider's hands, either. One is about as bad as the other.

A refusal in the show ring and a refusal during schooling differ only in the amount of time the rider may take to discipline his horse.

Because of the time-allowed factor, it is best to quickly correct the horse with stick or spurs when he stops, then immediately make a small circle and rejump the fence. Big classes have been won time after time with a refusal (only three faults) beating a knockdown (four faults). The important thing to remember is not to incur time faults on top of the refusal penalty. In competition, winning is at stake, not the perfect schooling of the horse at that moment.

However, if the refusal puts the horse out of the ribbons, or if the purpose of the class is for schooling, then the rider should address the fence after the refusal and correct the horse with stick, spurs, or both while he is facing the fence. Here time is not a factor, and what matters most is to train the horse correctly, establishing a "go forward" attitude for the next attempt. In the show ring, a rider is either trying to win or training his horse, or both; he should never waste a class by just "going for a ride."

A runout is something very different from a refusal. In this case, the horse has learned to duck out of the fence and escape. Again, in the show ring, if there is any possibility of being placed, don't waste time. Just circle back and jump the fence as quickly as possible. However, that is not a good correction for a runout; if anything, it will reinforce the habit. The way to discipline a horse and punish a runout is with a sharp jab in the mouth and a turn opposite the direction the horse ran out. (If a horse runs out to the right, turn him sharply to the left.) Then return and address the fence, and if necessary, use the stick and/or spurs. If you are having problems with a horse that stops or runs out, remember to go slower and keep the horse well in hand. The faster you go, the faster a horse will stop or run out.

Refusals or runouts may be a rare, unfortunate occurrence, but they can also be habits that can develop into a real vice. Habitual stopping or running out can be caused by a number of problems. The most likely cause is that the horse has been given a poor or weak ride. Perhaps he has been hit in the mouth, or he has gotten in wrong to his fences, or his rider sat back in the air and caused him to hit fences. Usually hesitation on the horse's part can be traced back to bad riding or bad training. Some horses, though, are green and lack confidence, or are just "chicken." Unfamiliar or spooky fences may cause them to stop or run out. Other horses will stop when they meet a certain kind of wrong distance to a fence—a little too long or too short for them. We should remember that horses don't love to jump, and unless we know what we are doing, they can all too easily learn to stop or to run out; this can become a confirmed habit very quickly. Any time a horse does not want to go forward and do his job—that is, jump—I take the matter most seriously. Runouts and refusals must be nipped in the bud.

The American Jumping Style is known for an ability to go fast against the clock. Here is where jump-offs and speed competitions are won or lost. We have a system and style that is best known for riding forward. Of course, it is essential for both horse and rider to be well schooled and comfortable jumping off sharp turns, angles, and roll-backs. The English are historically the best "turners" in the world; the Americans are not far behind.

As I have said, when walking the course for a class, a competitor must at that time walk the course for the jump-off, too. This is his only opportunity to predetermine the lines, striding, and turns that he must make in order to win. It is during the course walk that his plans are made. Of course, going later in a jump-off is a distinct advantage. One gets to see the others' strategy and to identify what needs to be done, where strides can be left out, and what turns to make in order to be competitive. It is imperative to watch other riders' rounds (or at least to have someone you trust watch them and report back to you) before your turn.

The most common mistake in riding a jump-off is going too slow.

Many people do not really know what going fast is; they don't want to go fast enough to win. Believe it or not, many people don't really want to win. For these riders, the best thing to do is give them lots of "fast" exercises, tight turns, sharp angles, roll-backs, and literally galloping to fences. It is up to the teacher to shake this kind of rider up, "put the fear of God into him," and try to get his blood up. Only an aggressive, go-for-broke attitude wins the jump-offs!

Years ago, Frank Chapot, one of our greatest Olympic riders and among the best speed riders of all time, taught me a great lesson: go as fast to the first fence as to the last fence. This sets the pace and rhythm for a jump-off or a speed class. It gets the rider's blood up. Often people go what they think is fast, but is not really fast, to the first fence. Many classes can be won by applying this lesson.

The other common error is going too fast—the rider who hurries, "foams at the mouth," and loses all thought and judgment of the horse and his balance. Usually these are green but overly aggressive people who at least are trying hard to win. (Of course, a few are forever stupid!) They need to learn to calm down, concentrate, and focus their determination. A really great jump-off round is so relaxed and under control that it feels almost slow, even though it is really fast. Katie Monahan-Prudent could go faster and look slower than any other rider I can think of. It takes a combination of talent and experience to be able to do that.

Horses have to learn how to jump at speed. I school my horses with a certain amount of pace, so jump-offs or speed classes are not such a big shock to them. It is going against the clock in the ring that really teaches horses how to gallop, turn back, and angle fences.

The American Jumping Style is shown at its best advantage over a technically difficult course. Just jumping mammoth single fences does not do our style justice. But a big course with related distances, solid fences, airy fences, natural fences, turns, broken lines, combinations, and a tight time allowed gives the American Jumping Style the edge. When I go to an international competition, I'm always relieved to see a "rider's course," not just a horse contest. Because of our equitation background, which revolves around technical precision, we have no trouble competing indoors. In fact, after the American string of wins in the World Cup Finals, many people were convinced that we were better indoors. That isn't exactly true. It was not so much the indoor environment, but the fact that everything came up quickly and all the distances were related on an indoor course, which we were used to. Now everybody has learned this precision, so nobody has an edge.

Every course designer has his own ideas, and each one will be somewhat different in his approach. Nevertheless, the questions asked by *all* good course builders are essentially the same. Will the horse go forward and lengthen his stride? Can he come back and shorten his stride? Is he bold to an imposing, spooky, or water obstacle? Is he careful over an airy, delicate, or flimsy fence set on flat cups? Does he turn left and right smoothly and softly, and does he jump equally well off both leads? Does he jump well at pace, or does he get rattled, flatten out, or get sloppy when asked to gallop and turn in order to make the time allowed? Does this horse know how to jump combinations? Combinations especially show off a really good horse and expose a limited horse.

I will describe a typical "ideal" short course for an indoor ring. This course would suit an open jumper or a Grade A horse. The start and finish markers are easy to get to; they are on the track of the course and would be hard to miss. A standard pace of about 350 meters per minute is needed to make the time allowed. This pace is also needed to jump the first line in six strides on a continuing stride. Seven strides would be possible, but this would waste time, complicate things, and be more effort for the horse.

The first fence has an ample ground line in front, something like

An Ideal Course to Demonstrate the American Jumping Style

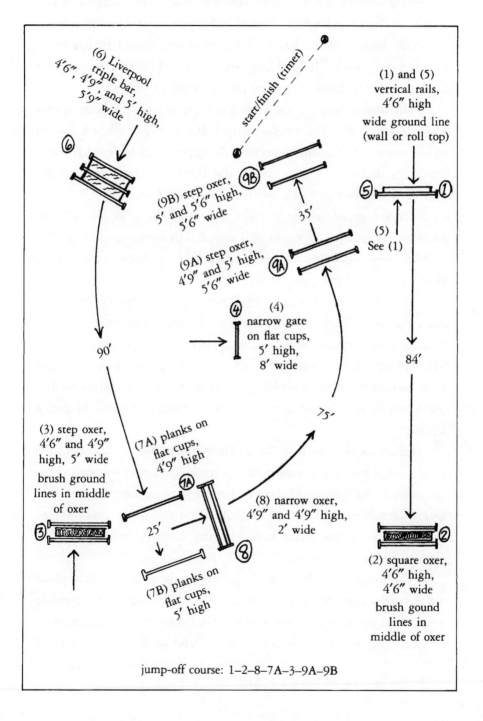

(6) Liverpool triple bar, 4'6", 4'9", 5'9" and 5' high, wide

(9B) step oxer, 5' and 5'6" high, 5'6" wide

(9A) step oxer, 4'9" and 5' high, 5'6" wide

start/finish (timer)

(1) and (5) vertical rails, 4'6" high

wide ground line (wall or roll top)

(5) See (1)

35'

84'

90'

75'

(4) narrow gate on flat cups, 5' high, 8' wide

(3) step oxer, 4'6" and 4'9" high, 5' wide brush ground lines in middle of oxer

(7A) planks on flat cups, 4'9" high

25'

(8) narrow oxer, 4'9" and 4'9" high, 2' wide

(7B) planks on flat cups, 5' high

(2) square oxer, 4'6" high, 4'6" wide brush gound lines in middle of oxer

jump-off course: 1–2–8–7A–3–9A–9B

a very low wall or roll top. It is almost a "free" fence jumped in this direction; there is no risk in jumping it. Fence number two, though not especially high or wide, has a false ground line caused by the brush boxes in the center. The problem here is to ride forward enough to get the six strides without overriding the front rail of the oxer.

The turn to fence three is long; it is an easy turn, making it easy to get to this rather big, ascending oxer. It is better to allow a smooth gallop to provide the impulsion for this scopey oxer, rather than use a lot of leg and spur. Again, watch the front rail. The brush in the middle of the oxer provides another false ground line.

Fence number four, at five feet, is not only high but also a "careful" fence (a gate on flat cups), and trappy. The turn comes up quickly and will surprise a horse, and the gate is narrow. A horse could run out here, or he could just jump badly.

On to fence number five—fence number one jumped in the opposite direction. This is probably a related distance from fence four, just as fence four is related to fence three. Here, that is not so important. The difficulty with this fence is that it is a false ground line. The rider must support the horse with his hands here, not throw him away. The horse may be a little out of balance on the turn, and he could drop a leg.

Fence number six is set on a diagonal opposite the corner of the ring. This is big, wide, and spooky, a triple bar Liverpool with water underneath. To compound the problem, it is going away from the in-gate. Horses here tend to drop back of the bit and get behind the legs. One could anticipate a stop here, or a rail down behind. It is best to plan to override this jump.

The ninety-foot distance to a combination of two vertical plank fences on flat cups (fences seven A and B) would be covered in a steady seven strides on a nearly straight line, or a shorter eight strides on more of a bending line. One cannot be too careful or slow to this type of fence, especially in a combination. At this particular double, one must underride and jump most delicately.

The roll-back to fence eight is designed to catch a time fault. The rider must turn promptly right back, yet without hurrying his horse. In a way, this is the hardest turn on the course to ride well.

Fence number eight is a high but narrow oxer. Jump this fence like a big vertical. Support the horse's front end with your hands; stay off his back during the flight of the jump.

The seventy-five-foot distance to the last oxer combination (fences nine A and B) will be easily made in five continuing strides. There would be no point at all in making six strides; this would just take away the impulsion. The rider must accurately control the track as well as the stride. A bigger horse should stay wider and a small horse a little closer to the inside of the track.

These last two oxers will ride big but not too long. The rider must ride for the scope of the last two fences (his horse will be tired by now), but at the same time, he must hold the horse together inside the combination.

When you are walking and planning a course, this is how detailed things get. Not only must you know how to plan a ride like this; you must then get on and do it!

Let's look at the jump-off course. Fence one to fence two could conceivably be an option. On a big-going horse, one could gallop fast to fence one and leave out a stride, doing five strides to fence two. If I were on a small horse, or if I didn't think I could turn well afterward, I'd do the six strides, but not on a straight line. In order to gallop fence one, I'd have to ride to fence two on a broken line. In either case, at that rate of speed I'd have to hold my horse off the front rail of fence two; it's still a false ground line.

No matter which striding option I've taken, I will have to make a good turn to fence eight. Fence seven B has been removed, so the turn must be tight—as tight as it must be to fence seven A. Fence seven A is on flat cups, so it would be best to make a tight turn but not override it at all. Almost any rub at all at this fence will cause a knockdown.

Fence three is a big oxer, so you'll have to give yourself a little room and time here. It's not a fence to take for granted and just turn back to. You've got to get across that back rail.

There is a little room to gallop to the last combination. It might be ridden as a related distance in a given number of strides. No matter what, some time must be made here. The course designer may have raised the last two fences and made them really big, forcing the horse and rider to concentrate on jumping them clean. This might be more of a riding problem than you think. Remember how short this combination might ride at this pace. A short distance to a high and wide fence at a gallop is always a good test of riding and jumping ability.

The timers are right after the last fence. Always take particular note of the location of the timers. This is even more important for speed classes and jump-offs.

Courses may be careful, scopey, or technical. Nowadays they are often a combination of all three—big, tricky to ride, or hard to jump clean. Very few horses in the world are very clean jumpers, have enormous jumping ability, *and* are tractable to ride.

Most horses need to be kept careful. A very sensitive, thin-skinned horse that hates to hit fences might only need to "toe" a big vertical just before going into the ring. Another, less careful jumper might need to jump a fence with a bamboo offset. This is constructed by placing a bamboo pole on brackets six inches to a foot higher than the top rail, on the takeoff side. This creates, in effect, a false ground line. A truly sloppy jumper actually needs to be hit, on occasion, with a bamboo pole. Such manual poling is not cruel, as some people think. Done with care by an expert, this method of poling can make a sloppy, potentially dangerous jumper into a good, safe performer. It is certainly kinder than a wreck!

Of course, everyone knows or at least suspects that there are other, more extreme methods of "sharpening up" a jumper, bordering on the inhumane. These extremes always backfire and, rather than enhancing performance, ruin it. I'm always happy that these extremists never really succeed in the long run. They never stand the test of time, and if they manage to get a horse to the top, it never lasts. They beat themselves!

There is a saying in show jumping: "No scope, no hope!" Scope means the horse's ability to jump big, wide fences, and big combinations with long distances. Some horses are born with great scope. Others develop it through their "try" and big heart. For major Grand Prix, World Cups, and championships, and the Olympic Games, a big-jumping horse is a must. A real trier that can't quite handle the biggest fences will eventually come to grief and give up. He might be a great everyday winner, but not, as a rule, an Olympic horse. A really big-time horse should be saved for those courses and classes. It is a shame to see a horse like that wasted over courses that don't really count.

There is almost no such thing in today's show jumping arena as a nontechnical course. We have to be able to go high, wide, short, long, angles and turns, and related distances. So a very careful or very scopey horse is not really useful anymore if he does not let the rider really ride and direct him. If you have little or no control, you have nothing.

In the old days, there were few riding problems to solve on most courses. Fences were big but simple, and technical problems were almost nonexistent. The "freak" jumpers and wild "rang-a-tangs" could win quite a lot if they could only jump high and clean. Nowadays most horses have to be quite tractable and rideable, and show jumping is a rider's game.

Today the best horses are very careful jumpers (but not so careful that they are "chicken-hearted"), have big enough scope, and are reasonably rideable. If a horse is a little short on one of these qualities, you can get by with him; if he is short in two departments, you are in trouble. Of course, if you doubt he is careful enough, he lacks scope, and he is hard to ride, I'd say forget him, even for minor league showing.

In short, riding a course, especially in actual competition, is something special and unique to itself, really the culmination of all the homework that has gone before. Always expect to lose some of the perfection you had in your schools at home; this is due to horse show distractions, pressure, and varying conditions. That is why it is so important to be well prepared and to be so very thorough in your work at home. If you are more than prepared, even if some degree of your perfection is bound to be lost, you will still have what you need to jump a course well when it counts—in competition.

Chapter 10

~

The American
Jumping Style in
Competition

~

The American Jumping Style permeates every division and every level we have in this country for hunters, jumpers, and hunter seat equitation. It has even pervaded worldwide show jumping and eventing, to some extent. This is a wonderful thing for riding and jumping in general, because this style of riding is based on very classical concepts.

To understand the American Jumping Style, one must understand how North American horse show competition works. Our hunter and hunter seat equitation divisions are unique; historically they were a foundation for the American Jumping Style, and they continue to be an essential element in our success. Our show jumping competitions and Grand Prix have evolved into something much closer to those found in England and Europe, but even so, they retain an American character, which both creates and shows off the American Jumping Style. To some degree, the same also applies to eventing, especially to our approach to the stadium jumping phase.

Judges and Judging and Their Effect on the American Jumping Style

The judging of our hunters and equitation riders has been a great factor in the development and evolution of the American Jumping Style. No other country judges hunters and riders on the "picture" they present as we do. North American hunter and equitation judges (most of whom also judge jumpers, too) must understand form and function. They must develop an eye for details—not superficial nit-picking, but the subtle and important clues to sound fundamentals. In this the judge's role is much like that of a dressage judge. Yes, our hunter and equitation judging is subjective; it leaves room for judges' opinions and preferences. However, those opinions and preferences must be based on experience, knowledge, and observation, and they must stay within the rules. Our hunter and equitation competition today has become so extensive and so sophisticated that it demands qualified and competent judging.

It is because of these divisions, and the fact that they are judged subjectively, that people in this country work so hard on their own and their horses' style. What a wonderful basis for all jumping: form first, rather than height or speed! Because of this factor, the drive for perfection and detail is built into our horsemanship; it is part of our psyche. We learn early and never forget that a horse must jump in form with a round bascule, use his knees, and be very rideable. A rider must keep his heels down and his eyes up, must avoid excess motion and use smooth "invisible" aids, yet must control his horse precisely and get a nearly perfect distance at every fence to have a hope of a ribbon. And both horse and rider must be spotlessly clean and correctly turned out. The judge is always watching and scoring every facet of our performance. We grow up anticipating and then respecting a judge's opinion of our own and our horse's performance and the overall picture we present.

On the other hand, judges (particularly equitation judges) have a great responsibility to the American Jumping Style and to our riders. Because riders, teachers, and trainers must and will tailor their riding and training to what judges will pin, judges and judging can have a profound effect on horsemanship, for better or worse. Good, educated judging, based on solid experience and classical principles, perpetuates good style and sound riding and training. However, the wrong kind of judging can allow fads and mannerisms to get out of hand, to the detriment of true, functional style and really good riding. Judges, especially in the equitation division, must keep our developing riders on the "straight and narrow."

Let's take a closer look at the various North American horse show divisions and how they contribute to the American Jumping Style.

Hunter Classes

Hunter classes, as they are known in North America, must be considered the very basis of the American Jumping Style. Without our unique hunter division, we would never have had our hunter seat equitation division, nor our stylish way of riding jumpers.

The characteristics of our hunter division—its horses, courses, performance, and way of riding—are very specific indeed. The show hunter must be of Thoroughbred type; a half-bred, heavy warmblood or draft cross will not have the quality and the type of movement to be competitive, no matter how well he jumps. A show hunter is judged on his jumping style, way of going, manners, and ability to maintain an even pace over a course of at least eight hunter-type fences. These are "fly" fences: simple verticals and oxers, with a natural appearance that simulates fences found in the hunting field. Post and rails, brush, gates, walls, coops, and aikens are typical; banks and ditches, which used to be found on outside hunt courses, are rare today. The fences are of medium height; in national competition they range from three feet six inches (green hunters, junior, and amateur hunters) to four feet (open hunters). There are also hunter classes with appropriate fence heights for small, medium, and large pony hunters, children's hunters, and special modified classes for very green horses.

Courses are designed to favor smoothness, accuracy, and a flowing performance. Because of the time constraints of getting so many entries through the day, courses today have been quite drastically shortened and tightened up, especially when they are held in indoor rings instead of over an outside course. The distances are closely related (indeed, measured with a tape measure) and are based on a standard stride of twelve or thirteen feet. Riders do not walk the course, because they know what the distances will be and that there will be no surprises. Therefore, the requirements include not only smooth riding, but as close to total control as possible. The horse must set a certain pace and keep it, jumping out of his stride and arriving at a perfect "spot" for each fence, neither too short nor too long. He must show excellent jumping form—folding his legs well, using his body, head, and neck in a good bascule, and jumping with an even arc. He must bend correctly around his turns and make perfect flying changes, and he must perform with good manners: without pulling, throwing his head, or resisting. He must do all this while appearing easy to ride, and the aids must be invisible. Any lengthening or shortening of stride should be so smooth and gradual as to be invisible.

In order to show a hunter off to his best advantage, the rider needs to be in a forward, galloping seat, not riding behind the motion. This position presents the best picture and makes it look as though horse and rider are moving effortlessly together. The rider's aids should be invisible; the judge or spectator should not see any obvious use of the hands, legs, or weight, nor should any use of the voice, spurs, or whip be apparent. For this reason, a light, sensitive, and athletic blood horse succeeds best as a hunter; a heavy, cold horse necessitates too much obvious riding.

Good style is a matter of necessity when showing hunters. Producing eight perfect jumps requires an accurate eye; the rider cannot check or drive obviously to get his horse to the right "spot." Therefore, he must be able to use his aids smoothly and accurately to make minute and invisible adjustments of stride. Since the horse's form in the air is judged, the rider must be in excellent balance in order to allow his horse the freedom of back, head, and neck to jump "round" with a good bascule. This requires a sound and classical position and sensitive use of the hands over the fence. Finally, even though the horse, not the rider, is being judged, an attractive rider in classical style makes any horse look better and easier to ride.

You can see why riding hunters using the American Jumping Style is most beneficial as a foundation for riding jumpers. Of course, the seat-of-the-pants, go-for-broke attack mentality is missing and must be gained elsewhere to round out the jumper rider's ability (another reason why it is so important for riders to be versatile and not just specialists). But there is no substitute for this smooth and classical approach to riding a course of fences that is hard to acquire in any other way than by riding hunters over hunter courses. In fact, many of our best international show jumping riders insist on continuing to show hunters just to maintain their smoothness and "eye" while working out of a galloping pace.

Hunter Seat Equitation

For the better part of the century, not only have hunter classes been the popular mainstay of North American horse shows, but so have hunter seat equitation classes, which developed along with the hunter division to provide a training platform for our young riders.

In equitation, only the rider is judged, although the horse's performance is credited to (or blamed on!) the rider's ability. The rider is judged on his position, seat, use of the aids, control of his horse, performance of the class requirements, and all-around horsemanship and style in general. The idea is to find the rider who best combines the ability to ride his horse with style and elegance while doing so. Equitation classes are held on the flat at walk, trot, and canter, or over fences ranging from about two feet six inches to approximately three feet six inches (depending on the age and experience of the riders). Competitors may also be required to perform individual tests drawn from a list of tests approved by the American Horse Shows Association, our national federation.

While equitation classes were originally limited to riders under the age of eighteen, they have become so popular that there are now adult equitation classes; equitation classes now range from short stirrup (for children under ten) to adult amateur equitation. The culmination of the hunter seat equitation division for junior riders (those who have not reached their eighteenth birthday) are three championships held in the autumn each year: the American Horse Shows Association Hunter Seat Medal Finals; the ASPCA Maclay Finals; and the USET Equitation Finals. The first two are quite similar in that they are both judged over a difficult and demanding hunter/jumper type course of three-foot six-inch fences. The main difference is that the ASPCA Maclay Finals are judged 50 percent on the flat at a walk, trot, and canter, and 50 percent on the rider's performance over fences; the

Hunter Seat Finals do not require flatwork. The USET Finals, how-ever, are quite different, judged in five phases: on the flat (requiring counter-canter and extended trot and canter as well as walk, trot, and canter); cavalletti; gymnastic jumping; a jumper-type course of fences up to three feet nine inches; and, finally, the top four competitors exchange horses and ride over fences again. To qualify for any of these championships, a rider must have won a minimum number of qualify-ing classes. The winners are considered to be the best junior riders in the country; many have gone on to a place on the U.S. Equestrian Team. To qualify, to ride in the finals, to place, or maybe even to win one of these championships is the dream of every North American youngster who ever jumps a fence.

Most of our famous stars of the U.S. Equestrian Team, including Olympic medalists from Bill Steinkraus to Conrad Homfeld, have won one or more of the national equitation finals. It is the exception rather than the rule to go on to the USET without first having won or at least placed high in one or more of these national equitation champion-ships.

Years of training, practice, and competing go into the making of these young equitation stars. They must have an extremely good foun-dation both on the flat and over fences. They should possess a good knowledge of all-around horsemanship, and they must have the right horse for the job. Equitation riders must work seriously on their seat and their style, putting in hours of exercises and work with and without stirrups. They must be capable of getting a smooth, correct, and precise performance from their horses; just "sitting pretty" is not enough! Much time must be spent on flat work and on developing an ability to school and improve a horse for performing tests and demanding courses. Equitation riders usually compete in the hunter division as well as equitation for additional experience; many also ride in the junior jumper division.

The AHSA equitation tests must be performed flawlessly with precision and smoothness. It is hard to describe to the uninitiated just how difficult these classes are to perform well in: besides turning in a correct and polished performance, a horse and rider must be turned out to perfection, which puts a premium on thorough preparation and attention to details. No doubt our success during the 1980s in the World Cup Finals in indoor ring conditions was due in part to our riders' training and experience competing in our equitation division. I have never seen anything quite like it anywhere else in the world.

It is fair to say that without the hunter division and the hunter seat equitation division, both unique to North America, the American Jumping Style as we know it would not exist today. The effects of these divisions have spread worldwide through the American Jumping Style of our jumper riders. The progression of jumping riders in North America is unique. Unlike riders in any other country in the world, young American riders do not begin their careers riding in jumper competitions. Rather, they start out by competing in junior hunter and hunter seat equitation divisions, and they only move on to showing jumpers once their fundamentals are well established.

To ride hunter and equitation classes successfully, one must have good basics, possess good style, and be able at all times to ride in an effective, workmanlike, but elegant way. Without the pressure to jump higher, wider, and faster, which is where one develops bad habits, the emphasis is on smooth but effective riding. What could be better? It is only when equitation riding becomes the be-all and end-all, and the tail begins to wag the dog, that this approach starts to lose its purpose. The danger is that riders and their coaches will get sidetracked into fads and mannerisms that have nothing to do with the basic principles of effective riding. Riding jumpers and developing a broad base of experience with many kinds of horses are what keep equitation riders true to the principles of the American Jumping Style.

Once a young rider has mastered the fundamentals necessary to compete over hunter and equitation courses, he is ready to begin showing in junior, amateur-owner, or preliminary jumper classes. Relatively speaking, these divisions do not have very big fences, but they offer the same technical problems as the higher jumper divisions. The wonderful thing about this progression is that a young rider is technically ready, once he starts riding jumpers, to execute the courses with knowledge and confidence. Definitely not the "rough and ready" approach, this progression produces good young riders and stylists en masse.

Yes, it is necessary, as time goes on, to acquire some "seat of the pants" experience and to experience the "blood and guts" of the jumper world. But that is easy to do. Those who will make it to the top will accept the challenge and survive; what is more, they will survive with their style intact. The rider who starts out by learning to survive in the jumper ring without the equitation base of style will never be as good a stylist, and often he is not as good a rider, especially on hot, sensitive horses.

This progression has been such a sound system of development for us that other countries around the world are starting to incorporate equitation and working hunter classes into their horse shows. (Working hunter classes compete over fences, while in many countries, hunter classes are judged under saddle and/or on the line.) Foreign horsemen see the tremendous value of starting correctly, not only for their young riders but for their young horses. Our consistent and continued success in producing good, stylish riders for international jumping competition must be largely attributed to this sound beginning.

Jumper Classes

The evolution of jumper classes in North American horse shows over the past fifty years has been most interesting and instrumental in the development of our jumping horsemanship. Without this evolution —something most other countries have not gone through—our American Jumping Style and ability to ride jumpers would not be the same.

The early American jumping competitions revolved around jumping clean, mostly over big vertical fences. Spread fences, although found on some courses, were not emphasized, nor was speed much of a factor. The name of the game was to jump high poles, gates, or panels without a rub. Most classes were conducted under "touch" rules—a front leg touch counted one fault, and a hind leg touch was half a fault. A front knockdown was four faults and a hind knockdown two faults; a first refusal was three faults, the second refusal six faults, and the third meant elimination. There was no maximum "time allowed"; one could pull up to a trot or even a walk between fences as long as forward movement was maintained. Two popular classes were "touch and out" (in which a horse was eliminated when he touched a fence) and "knockdown and out" (the horse was eliminated at the first knockdown). In all classes, tied horses jumped off over raised obstacles, but time was not a factor, even in jump-offs. Width, combinations, and time were not terribly important in the old days—it was jumping high and clean that counted.

What did these early classes teach American horsemen? Two things. First was control. One had to have a horse under control, well in hand, and very collected in order to jump those big, airy verticals clean. Second was the ability to jump fences very cleanly. This special skill on the rider's part is often overlooked today, with so many classes against the clock. A really good jumper rider must know how to get a horse to jump pretty nearly "rub free." In my opinion, the riders who grew up in English-speaking countries riding "rub" classes had a great learning advantage. The days of these competitions are well over; nonetheless, the early classes were a good riding exercise.

Gradually, during the late fifties and early sixties, as the U.S. Equestrian Team grew in popularity and Bertalan de Némethy rose to prominence as a trainer, horse shows began to offer classes run closer to international FEI rules. Bonus point stake classes and junior as well as senior "Olympic-style" competitions began to appear. Time allowed and timed jump-offs were introduced, and spread fences, combinations, and related distances in lines of fences were emphasized. By the mid-1960s, this direction was clearly the way to go, and horse shows and course designers as well as riders and trainers all saw the wave of the future. Pamela Carruthers, the great English course designer, did a lot for North American riding and training—building big, bold, wide fences, often on a long stride, that got us going forward and thus allowed our horses to develop scope.

By the time of the 1970s and 1980s, FEI-style courses and rules were the norm for North America. Rub classes were nearly extinct (a fact which I personally have mixed emotions about). Now the trend seemed more and more to be toward FEI competitions, with the focus on the weekly and weekend Grand Prix or World Cup class. This emphasis has made our status in the world jumping community stronger than ever. We were able to beat the best in Europe on any given day, something that had been virtually impossible for any except our most seasoned USET riders just a couple of decades ago.

The evolution of these different stages of jumper competition has been good for us. It taught us not so much about style (our hunters and equitation classes taught us that), but more about control, precision, accuracy, timing, striding, and speed. Thanks to our progression from one stage to another, we've had a chance to learn it all.

Grand Prix competitions have now proliferated all over North

America. The number and size of competitions, the prize money, and the number of entries have increased tremendously. There is also a range of jumper divisions to develop horses and riders at various levels —schooling, modified, preliminary, intermediate, junior, and amateur-owner jumpers, to name a few—as well as a strong commercial market for proven jumpers and talented jumper prospects.

For the past twelve to fifteen years, the European sport horse, or warmblood, has played an important part in the showing scene here in North America. With recent changes in the economics of the racing scene, it has become more and more difficult to acquire sound, suitable Thoroughbred horses off the race track at a reasonable price. In the past, not only were more Thoroughbreds or seven-eighths-breds raised for the hunting field and show ring, but there were more race horses and fewer tracks. The less successful racers had no place to go, so we horse show people got a chance at them before they became physical or mental cripples. Today, with many more race tracks and racing days, a horse must be pretty well washed up before he is no longer any use on the track. As this great source of Thoroughbreds for the jumping sports dwindled, the European supply of jumping stock filled the void. There has been a rush to import warmbloods as trained jumpers, jumper prospects, dressage horses, and other sport horses; now, out of other necessities, the pendulum must swing back.

The recent trend toward using warmbloods has most definitely affected our style of riding, and not for the better. It has put us "behind the motion" in a driving seat. While I'm not so enthusiastic about what riding warmbloods has done to our style, I must say that this type of horse has taught us a lot about riding, especially on the flat. It is interesting to note that the continental warmblood horse requires dressage, likes dressage, and flourishes on dressage. One cannot succeed with this type of horse without understanding the rudiments of flat work. Thoroughbreds are different. With Thoroughbreds, one needs to compromise and often skirt the dressage issue; really intensive dressage is not usually necessary. North American riders never really understood or appreciated the art of dressage until the warmblood horse forced us to do so.

On the other hand, seeing our riders back on their buttocks, with their upper bodies on (and even behind) the vertical, often body-riding and pumping away at their horses, is not my idea of style. This approach is almost mandated by the heavier, colder warmblood horse, but fortunately, most Americans are not buying these heavier types any more. They learned their lesson the hard way—by having to live, ride, and win with these beasts!

And so, in short, I'd have to say that the warmblood jumper has been a part of the recent evolution of our horsemanship in this country. Hopefully, the good we've learned from these horses, especially about the use of dressage, will outweigh the bad things they have done to our classical style: the tendency toward overriding and getting behind the motion. I do not want to see the American Jumping Style of riding jumpers change into something other than what brought us our greatest success. And I'm sure that when the pendulum swings back toward the Thoroughbred horse, our horse of choice, this will not happen. It is up to the professionals in this country to have "blood" horses available for their students and to teach them how to ride such horses correctly. I will always equate "style" with "lightness." And to be able to ride "light," one must have a light-type horse. The Thoroughbred or near-Thoroughbred is that type of horse.

The USET and
International Competition

The U.S. Equestrian Team (USET) really came into prominence in the early fifties, when people were getting back on their feet after the Second World War. Our earliest civilian Olympic team was organized to fill the gap left by the demise of the U.S. Army equestrian teams. Bert de Némethy took over the training of the jumping squad in 1955; it was then that things really took hold. In those days, his game was the only game in town, and everybody wanted to be on a winning team—as an owner, a rider, or even a groom. And his was a winning team!

Bert de Némethy is the man most universally given credit for the American Jumping Style. All in all, this is a fair assessment in terms of international competition. He was, however, given riders with sound basics and great style—riders produced by such prominent American teachers as Gordon Wright, Cappy Smith, Jimmy Williams, Vladimir Littauer, and Jane Marshall Dillon. Position and style, as well as "spit and polish" and good stable management, were very important to de Némethy. He was a classicist from head to toe, and he tried to instill that in all his students.

While flat work (or dressage) had gradually been taking hold during this era, Bert de Némethy made it the *sine qua non* for the jumping horse. Through his devotion to classical dressage methods, he even had a tremendous impact on the hunters in the decades ahead, as well as the jumpers and equitation riders. Impulsion, flexion, bending, half-halts, and lateral work were all relatively new concepts in those good old days. Bert changed all that.

Bert de Némethy's use of cavalletti, trotting fences, and gymnastic jumping was presented to us really for the first time. Most of us had never seen open jumpers trot quietly over poles on the ground to a five-foot fence—and jump it with a foot to spare! I well remember how American horsemen stood dumbfounded and unbelieving, watching this man work, when he first came over here. Remember that most of the open jumpers before de Némethy went like wild "rang-a-tangs"; most were forcibly "rated" into their fences. Many, too, were overbitted; a jumper that went quietly in a snaffle was rare as a day in June!

With the coming of de Némethy, the USET jumping squad changed from a competition team of very capable, representative individuals to a structured, disciplined group of young horsemen and -women that became the force to be reckoned with at any show in the world. Not only were de Némethy's teams noted for style, but they could readily win Nations Cups and Grand Prix. (In fact, if they hadn't been winners, nobody might have cared very much about their style!) Never before or since the de Némethy years—from 1955 through 1980 —has the USET jumping team had such *esprit de corps*. True, U.S. riders have won a great deal in the last ten years, but the whole package is not the same, nor will it ever be quite the same again. Change and evolution are sometimes for the best, but not always.

Eventing and the American Jumping Style

Event riders have trod almost the same path as our jumping riders over the last sixty years. First it was Fort Riley and the Forward Seat of Caprilli, Saumur, and Chamberlin that showed its stamp. The Army teams between the two World Wars consisted of good stylists and sound horsemen who were incredibly versatile by today's standards. Major Harry Chamberlin, who won the individual silver medal in show jumping, was also a member of the winning three-day team at the 1932

Olympics. Who would even try that today? The cavalry influence carried over in eventing, much as with the jumpers, into the midfifties, when more influence was felt from Hungarian and German instructors who had emigrated to the United States. Stefan von Visy, a compatriot of Bertalan de Némethy, coached the three-day team through much of the 1960s with some success.

However, the highlight of our modern three-day event team arrived with the personage of Jack Le Goff in 1970. Le Goff, a French Olympian himself, brought every aspect of good horsemanship with him. He is a superb rider, a brilliant teacher, a great all-around horseman, and most of all, a winner. Le Goff's touch produced nothing but success for the USET—especially gold and silver medals in the Olympics, World Championships, and Pan American Games. In my opinion, separating Jack Le Goff from our Olympic team was one of the biggest mistakes in our equestrian history, and the American record since he left has sadly proven this observation.

Jack Le Goff's school, the French School, and our original three-day event background (the Italian-French military Forward Seat) complemented each other perfectly. Le Goff reinforced what we knew to be correct position, use of aids, dressage, and jumping, and he emphasized the importance of good stable management and getting horses properly fit. With de Némethy on one side and Le Goff on the other, American riders of either jumping or eventing could be proud to be American. They went to any competition in the world during those "golden years" as the team to beat.

Today, the eventing world both uses and modifies the classic American Jumping Style. American eventers usually deal with the hot Thoroughbred horse (one which is fighting fit by the time he gets to competition!). Therefore, they need the sensitivity, balance, and tact that are indigenous to the American Jumping Style. However, the demands of cross-country riding at speed, including steeplechase obstacles, drop fences, and water and other cross-country obstacles, have led event riders to somewhat modify their position. Most eventers ride with a rounder back and often with the lower leg somewhat more forward than would be perfectly classic form; these modifications help riders cope with holding a strong horse at a gallop and jumping at speed. The eventer's cross-country seat often resembles more that of a steeplechase rider than the seat used by an equitation rider. In the stadium jumping phase, however, both the job to be done and the style in which it is best accomplished are pure American Jumping Style. Many of our top eventers also ride show jumpers or work with the top American jumping coaches. Since a rail down in the show jumping phase can determine a medal, the best eventers are using our time-honored methods to school their horses and refine their stadium jumping techniques.

Current Exponents of the American Jumping Style

All the great stylists in America today ride in a similar position. There are, of course, individual differences in some small details, but essentially the four parts of the rider's body—lower leg, base of support, upper body, and hands and arms—work the same. These stylists are all, to a greater or lesser degree, Forward Seat riders possessing a classical, educated leg, a light but deep seat, and a soft, following hand.

I'll mention only a few of the American riders who are winning today.

Joe Fargis comes to mind first, not only because he won the individual gold medal in the Prix des Nations at the 1984 Olympic Games, but also because he is so exemplary of the American Jumping Style. Joe is a pure and natural rider. His heels are down; his lower leg is on his horse; he leans forward in balance, looks ahead, relaxes his arms, and gallops and jumps. His position is uncomplicated and classical, tracing directly back through his work with Bert de Némethy, Jane Marshall Dillon, and Vladimir Littauer to the roots of our American Jumping Style. Joe is a classic Forward Seat stylist.

Michael Matz would probably win the world's stylist award. Horsemen from every continent think of him as the premier stylist in show jumping today. First of all, he and his horses are always turned out impeccably, with "spit and polish." He works his horses on the flat, via de Némethy's influence, in a more European way, an approach that appeals not only to the European jumping community, but to South Americans and North Americans as well. Michael combines his dressage work and jumping masterfully. He never loses his relaxed, forward movement in jumping, yet his flat work is there—a rare combination. When one thinks of style and show jumping, Michael's name is second to none.

Hap Hansen, an American rider from the West Coast, rides simply beautifully. He also rides very simply and naturally; nothing is made complicated. He would have to be considered one of America's greatest stylists today. Hap rides hundreds of different horses in competitions every year, and they all love his touch. Horses jump particularly well for him, even on short acquaintance. Again, he combines strength and power with softness and finesse.

Katie Monahan-Prudent has for years epitomized the American Jumping Style both at home and abroad, for both men and women riders. No one, and I mean *no one*, can ride under pressure like Katie and yet still retain her flawless position and use of invisible aids. She looks so smooth and effortless that it appears as if she is doing nothing. That is real art. And yet no one—man or woman—is stronger or more determined on horseback than Katie. She commands respect worldwide, and as a competitor she is feared by all. What's more, her style remains so correct that even years after leaving the junior ranks, she convincingly won the 1992 Equitation Hall of Fame competition.

Beezie Patton, a protégé of Katie Monahan-Prudent, is exemplary of the American Jumping Style. She has a beautiful position, rides smoothly with invisible aids, and is a winner in the ring. Beezie gallops forward on a soft rein and allows the horse to do the work. She accompanies and supports, yet when needed, she can be most powerful and dominate the situation.

Anne Kursinski, like Michael Matz, has combined her strong dressage background with that of American hunter riding. She is also very much appreciated by the Europeans because of her active, aggressive ride. Anne can ride any horse as well as or better than most men, and she can deal with the European Warmblood horse better than most women. Anne has a tremendous record winning internationally, as good as or better than any woman in the history of show jumping.

Rather than talk only about American riders who use the American Jumping Style, I'd like to point out some of the world's best riders who have been attracted to this way of riding and have incorporated it into their approach. (On a personal note, I have had some influence on all of these international horsemen through instruction and clinics.)

Ian Millar of Canada, twice a World Cup champion, rode effectively but without too much style in the 1972 Munich Olympic Games. When he came to work with me shortly afterward, I changed him dramatically by putting him on our show hunters. Ian became an instant success in the hunter ring, where he learned to lean forward, drop his heels, and work with invisible aids. For a man of his great height, he handles his conformation particularly well by controlling his angles.

Mark Todd, twice Olympic three-day event gold medal winner for New Zealand, lived in the United States for a year. He obviously liked this style of riding, which he demonstrates not only in eventing but also in show jumping. Mark is a particularly strong rider who likes to ride "soft"—what a wonderful combination! Like Ian Millar, he is a tall rider who uses his angles to advantage. He is a Forward Seat rider with beautiful hands and a great leg.

Thomas Fuchs and I started working together in the late 1970s. He was on the Swiss team at Madison Square Garden and had one particularly diffcult, hot, gray horse. I taught him to work with his voice (a cluck) rather than use such a strong leg. He became a devoted protégé of mine, both as a rider and as a teacher. Thomas is known for his galloping approach to fences, the forward inclination of his upper body, and his deep heels—all characteristics of the American Jumping Style.

Paul Darragh, an Irishman, is as meticulous and detailed a horseman as I ever met. We've worked together both here in the United States and in Europe. When one combines Paul's vast experience and work ethic with this kind of talent, it's hard to beat. I am very proud that Paul has not only incorporated the American Jumping Style into his own riding, but brought it to the whole of Ireland as well.

Jean-Claude Vangeenberghe is a Belgian rider who has chalked up a spectacular record over the past few years. He is the European rider I have worked most closely with on a private basis. A sensitive man, Jean-Claude can ride hot, difficult mares with great tact.

Competition and the Development of Young Riders in the American Jumping Style

In North America today, horse shows are an important part of a young rider's development and learning process, often from a very early stage. This is a double-edged sword. While our children learn right from the start to ride in good style and to present themselves and their horses well in competition, it can also lead to too much single-minded emphasis on showing only, without taking the time to develop a broad base in real horsemanship, which is the backbone of any lasting success.

A very young child (up to age ten or twelve) or a beginner should start out on a quiet pony or school-type horse. During this time, he should have fun on horseback—bareback riding, trails, cowboys and Indians, gymkhanas, and the like. He should also learn about taking care of his pony and good horsemanship. However, no matter how young he begins (and I don't recommend starting children younger than seven or eight), he should have good riding lessons. They should be short lessons, depending on the age of the child, but he should learn and practice position, use of the aids, simple schooling movements, and elementary jumping. This jumping can begin with an "imaginary jump"—a line drawn in the dirt, or a single ground pole. The important thing is to learn to do it right from the beginning.

For competition, children at this stage should be mounted on ponies or very quiet school horse–type mounts. They need to develop confidence and solid basics first; brilliance comes later! At this age, they should only compete in short stirrup classes, equitation classes for their age group, pony hunter classes, and children's hunter classes. In these classes, the fences are low, and there is plenty of opportunity to learn good style and develop good habits. These children are too young and too small to consider jumper classes or advanced horsemanship divisions, no matter how promising they may be. Their only concern (and their parents' and trainers') at this stage should be to become educated in a basic way about riding and all-around horsemanship.

Too many young children are scared, bored, or "turned off" at this stage by pushy parents and instructors. These adults should know better, but their egos get in the way. The better the talent I have to work with, be it in a young horse or a young person, the slower I go. I want to make sure that they are never scared, overfaced, or bored, and also that they have a broad-based, thorough, and very sound foundation.

Most children should outgrow ponies and move on to horses for children's hunters and junior hunters by the time they are twelve to fourteen years old, unless they are unusually short in stature or terribly timid. (A few short people can ride ponies forever!) Ponies are different from horses, especially from sensitive blood horses. Children can pick up bad riding habits on ponies that will take a long time to get rid of. The longer they ride ponies, the harder it may be to make the transition to a horse. Also, it is better psychologically for young people going into their teens to grow up and start riding horses. For these reasons, I do not like young riders to work with ponies for too long. In general, ponies are for very small children, period. Children should not stay on ponies too long!

The pony riders I have taught all made the move from ponies to horses very easily, if they have been taught correctly from the beginning, a horse is just a bigger animal, to be ridden the same way. The pony riders learned about hunters and how they should go from showing in the pony hunter and children's hunter divisions, and they had also been introduced to the idea of equitation classes.

By the time a young rider reaches his early teens, he should be ready to move into the junior hunter division and a more demanding equitation division. Now his concentration must be on good riding. Never again will his style on a horse be so carefully scrutinized. There are many, many good young riders with great style in this level of equitation; to compete, a rider simply must ride with good style and with some sophistication. This experience will stand him in good stead for the rest of his riding life. While the main emphasis of a young rider's development through most of his teenage years should be on hunters and equitation, I have no objection to including some jumper work (children's jumpers or junior jumpers) as long as he is physically and mentally ready. By the time my junior riders reach their late teenage years, I like most of them (with some exceptions) to have the experience of riding junior jumpers. A few very precocious riders even ride open jumpers at quite a young age; however, I do not recommend this except for the most exceptional talents.

The most difficult stage for a young horseman is between ages eighteen and twenty-five. When he must graduate out of the junior ranks at eighteen, he may feel like a fish out of water; he may be out of his depth in the regular classes open to all adults. The young rider division is a very good way to fill this void, both nationally and internationally. Nationally, the amateur-owner divisions (in both hunters and jumpers) also offer good experience at this level—to a point.

If I have a very gifted, precocious young rider, I do not let him ride in amateur divisions. This can lead him to start to think like an amateur, become "soft," and let down his edge; his riding will deteriorate. Instead, I enter him in all the divisions that the professionals ride in, be they hunters or jumpers. Not only is the competition tougher and the courses harder, but the environment is better for someone who may have the capability to go on to international riding or to become a professional horseman. While people are making the transition to the senior ranks, it is most important that they retain their style and their basics. Many riders at this stage, once they are out of the equitation division, let their riding really deteriorate.

Young riders and horsemen should not be cast adrift in the highly competitive horse world—no good will come of this. They should have older mentors until they are well into their twenties and have acquired a lot of experience—the right experience. Yes, by this time they should be making lots of decisions, and they will naturally make lots of mistakes. That doesn't matter. The good ones will learn from their mistakes.

Adults are either professionals or amateurs. Of course, some amateurs do have a professional mentality, and some professionals occasionally think or behave like amateurs, but the overall distinction is most important. A professional stakes his livelihood and his career on his decisions and his ability to produce. An amateur, however good and however dedicated, has a different motivation. So it is according to this amateur or professional mentality that we proceed, and whichever mentality we choose leads us to succeed in our own way. Of course, talent, horses, and money also have a great deal to do with how we plan our horse show career, what classes we enter, and what goals we set. But it is this all-important mentality that helps make these decisions for us. Always remember that no matter which direction you go in the horse business, style, taste, and class come first. That is how you are judged.

Putting the American Jumping Style to Work in Competition

When entering a show, whether you are an amateur or professional at any level, you must know which divisions and classes to enter. Equitation classes are judged on the rider; for the most part, they are for junior riders, but there are now adult equitation classes, too. Once riders are out of the very competitive junior equitation division, these classes serve best for the rider who cannot go on very far with his horse in either the hunter or jumper division.

The attractive, good-moving horse with a correct jumping style makes the hunter, while an average-moving horse with more jump, but perhaps of nondescript type, makes a jumper. Horses will usually find their own level and division at which they can shine, if you let them. Trying to make a horse into what he is not simply doesn't work.

It is always better to underface a horse than to overface him. If I don't know much about a certain horse, I'll start him out in an easy hunter division or the schooling jumper division. I can always move him up when I am more confident about his ability. Too often people—especially young people—want to upgrade horses and riders too quickly. This is the quickest and surest way to ruin a good thing. Take your time with both horses and riders!

Horses learn slowly, so keep them competing at a reasonable height for a good year before moving into a higher, wider, harder division. If you are not exactly sure what division and what classes your horse belongs in, be sure to ask someone who does know. There is nothing more distasteful at a horse show than to see a horse (or a rider) entered over his head, where he doesn't belong.

Hunter seat equitation riders should progress from one level of competition to the other in a natural and unhurried way as their riding improves. There are so many equitation classes tailored to a rider's age and grade of riding. As a rule, it is best to wait until your age requires you to move up into the next age group, or until you have won your way out of one restricted category (like maiden, novice, or limit), before attempting a higher one. You should win a few under-fourteen classes before entering the open equitation under eighteen. I usually prefer a rider to have won his way out of limit equitation before even trying Medal or Maclay classes. USET classes are even more difficult than Medal or Maclay classes. Don't rush them! You'll have fewer mental and physical setbacks by going one step at a time in equitation, rather than going for it all at once.

When one is riding advanced-level equitation classes, it is almost indispensable experience to enter junior jumper classes as well. The jumper division gives an equitation rider an added dimension of strength that the hunter and equitation divisions alone cannot provide. Showing hunters, equitation, and jumpers all at the same time gives a rider a background combining style and function that really cannot be found anywhere else in the world.

The best way to prepare mentally for a competition is to do your homework. Relaxation comes out of confidence. Confidence comes from knowing what to do and how to do it, especially when things go wrong. That is why experience is so important, especially in major championships, finals, or the Olympic Games. The really experienced people have "been around the block"; they have been up against pressure and know how to get out of trouble when it occurs. Green riders who have not yet experienced enough problems tend to fall apart under real pressure.

Confidence is a never-ending situation of building up or tearing down. Correct schooling at home, along with knowing how to progressively enter the appropriate classes and divisions in competition, can build people up to the top. One really bad school, or entering a class over one's head, can tear a horse or rider to shreds in a matter of minutes!

I cannot overemphasize the importance of going slowly and carefully with both the horse's and rider's schooling and preparation for horse shows. The greatest mistake most riders, teachers, and trainers make is rushing—pushing people and horses past their level of experience or competence.

Horses and riders can sometimes do things they logically should not be able to do simply because they are bursting with confidence. Once they have doubts and their confidence is shaken, then fear sets in and it is all over. The greatest art of a teacher, trainer, or rider is not only to instill confidence but to maintain it.

Today many riders in North America are studying sports psychology, and that is a good thing. However, I do believe that good teachers are born. Good teachers are part psychiatrist! In teaching, one learns and feels how to handle pupils' minds. And in competitive riding, the great champions learn how to handle their own minds. That is how they become champions. However, good reading, seminars, and more knowledge of this subject can only help.

As I have said, experience gives a rider the knowledge of what works and what to do when things go wrong. In competition, I'll always take experience over knowledge. Some people who ride know a lot but can't do a lot. Others know very little, but they've done a lot. Give me the latter when we are going to a horse show!

Knowledge, experience, and habit go hand in hand. It must be habit to wait on a horse that is rushing his jumps. It must be habit to correct a runout or a refusal properly. It must be habit to see a distance, and to be able to ride different kinds of distances and lines well. It must be habit to *know the rules of the competition* and to check details without getting confused. Again, it's the experienced, cool "old dog" that is best in the championships. He's encountered every possible problem many, many times before!

The best example of the American Jumping Style at work (especially before the whole world realized that it had something to learn from American riding) was the 1984 Olympic Games in Los Angeles. Yes, we did have the advantage of competing on our own turf and of already being familiar with Bert de Némethy's approach to training and courses. But it was the technology of the American Jumping Style that gave us a discernible edge. Out of our riders' position, use of the aids, flat work, bitting, gymnastics, course analysis, and show ring experience came our success. It was the American System that allowed us to field such an extraordinary "Dream Team" of horses and riders, and that really won those medals.

During the 1980s, we won the World Cup Finals again and again because of the American Jumping Style. Time after time the World Cup Finals standings reflected the consistency and sophistication of the American Jumping Style and system of riding. The Europeans were baffled; no one else was coming close. We had developed a precision and perfection that had never been seen before in the sport of show jumping. Our history, heritage, horsemanship, riders, teachers, trainers, vets, blacksmiths, course designers, judges—all contributed their part and all came together to put us on top. Now, of course, everyone to one degree or another has adopted the principles of this system. No single country will ever again so dominate the show jumping scene.

In conclusion, the American Jumping Style has now permeated and influenced every corner of the jumping sports. The small pony hunters at Devon, equitation riders at Harrisburg, junior jumper riders in Canada, show jumpers all across Europe, South America, and South Africa, the eventing teams of Australia and New Zealand—all of these jumping sports and riders have been touched by our system. It may show up in a better turned out horse and rider, or a superior braiding job. Perhaps it's better preventative veterinary care, or giving a horse more time turned out in a paddock. Or it might be a rider in a beautiful position having a double clear round in Belgium or Switzerland, or an event horse jumping round and carefully in the stadium jumping phase. Whatever the aspect of improvement, and whatever country or continent we are talking about, I am proud that our system has proven itself so valid and legitimate that it has made such contributions. The American Jumping Style crystallized all the theories and ideas that went before it, and, in fact, it has given them back to the rest of the world with some improvement.

Chapter 11

~

*The Future
of the American
Jumping Style*

~

I am worried about the future of the American Jumping Style. Perhaps it won't die, but by all appearances, it may decline. Producing style is like baking a cake—it takes just the right recipe. From the 1950s through the 1980s, we had the right recipe. Today, some of the ingredients are harder to find.

The American Jumping Style has always been based on the American Hunter Seat. Because of the constraints of time and the many shows that are held in indoor rings, the long, galloping courses and outside courses of yesteryear have given way to shorter courses with tighter distances. By eliminating those long, galloping outside hunter courses, we have lost something from our hunter divisions and, consequently, from the way we ride hunters. The real Forward Seat of old is disappearing, and that is a shame. Much of our great jumper riding was built upon the Forward Seat and the galloping courses it served so well.

Our society today—riders, teachers, and pupils—is not the same. The old values of discipline, hard work, and getting one's hands dirty have changed. Specialists exist in every field, and riders today don't have to do a little bit of everything. This makes them more limited and therefore weaker horsemen. It's a funny thing, but the more one does around the barn with his own hands and his own horse, the better rider he'll be in the ring.

Great teachers and great eras go together; they rise together. And the reverse is true—they decline together. I don't see many teachers coming along today to match the masters of old—de Némethy, Le Goff, Wright. A pupil is a reflection of his teacher, no more, no less. Of course, those old horsemen could do so much in so many different ways with horses. All were experienced in other disciplines; some even competed internationally in more than one discipline. Who does that today? Today, as I've said, things are too specialized, limited, and narrow. The teachers of today are not comprehensive enough, and their students are not getting a broad enough base.

Reading is so important. We used to have to read. Nowadays, too many people are lazy about reading horse books. There are good books on stable management, veterinary medicine, shoeing, conformation, dressage, jumping, and riding. There are also classics—books without which a rider's education is incomplete. It's essential to read some of everything in order to become a comprehensive horseman.

From the riding and training point of view, one must know and really understand the theory behind everything one does. Too many teachers today "parrot" what they see and hear without understanding the mechanics—the "whys"—or the basic principles behind a practice. You must always understand *why* you do a certain thing; you can't just do it. And this is one reason style is on the decline. Teachers, without reading and comprehensive knowledge of the basic principles, will sway with the different fads—high hands, low hands, toes in, toes out, lean forward, lean backward, and so on. Too many teach their students to copy mannerisms practiced by a winner in the hope that they too will produce a winner. Rather, they first must understand classical style, then adhere to it fanatically without waver or compromise. To produce style, an instructor must stamp his rider, and it must be a classic stamp. It takes knowledge, dedication, and lots of plain hard work!

Look what has happened in dressage today. Yes, there are lots of effective riders; they get the job done. But where is the style? Where are the invisible aids? As far as I can see, the style is all but gone. Stirrups are too long. Consequently riders are reaching for their stirrups, which raises their heels and loosens their legs. Without an effective lower leg, we see "body riding," or pumping, and riders way behind the motion of their horses, often behind the vertical. This position in turn goes along with a roached back and a bobbing head, and all too often with hands too low and eyes down. Go to any dressage show today, and you will see too much of this kind of riding. That is what has happened to style in the dressage community, but it didn't used to be that way. The dressage riders of the fifties, sixties, and seventies were much better stylists than most are today. That decline will happen in the jumping world, too, if we do not continue to teach along strictly classical lines. Teachers must be the watchdogs of history.

Style in riding, be it dressage or jumping, is a precious thing. It has evolved over many centuries and has been taught, practiced, and passed down to us by men who were smarter than we are. I've always felt it better to be a good copier than a poor innovator. Let's not fix what isn't broken, nor tamper with the foundation of all our riding success up until now. It would be a crime to lose our American Jumping Style and what it has stood for. We cannot let that happen.

We are fortunate to have, in this country, a truly marvelous and widely varied equestrian tradition, in which form and function have been so beautifully matched that our best riders have been supremely effective and supremely stylish at the same time. This tradition has helped us achieve successes on the world level that we hardly dared dream of when we first took on the European riders at their own equestrian games shortly after the turn of the present century. My fear that we will lose sight of this in the current do-it-yourself, do-your-own-thing era is tempered by the fact that all the ingredients are still there in abundance, if you seek them out—the horse talent and the riding talent, the written knowledge to develop them, and the spoken knowledge to teach it. We owe it to ourselves and to our wonderful tradition not to let these ingredients go to waste.

I am proud to have been considered an exemplar of the American Jumping Style, and I am lucky to have been able to teach it around the world for more than three decades. I am sure that if we remember to cherish this wonderful tradition and follow its precepts and ideals, we will be just as successful in the future as we have been in the past.

PART II

~

*Stable Management
and Show Presentation*

by Susan E. Harris

Author's Note:

I asked Susan Harris to contribute the final two chapters to this book, dealing with stable management and show turnout, because I consider these subjects to be inextricably related to the American Jumping Style, and because Susan knows more and writes better about them than anyone else.

I should point out, too, that the influence of the Americans on the Europeans has been almost as marked in this respect as it has in regard to riding style. When I was riding in Europe for the first time with the USET, we had some top show ring grooms with us, and our jumpers were turned out like conformation hunters. I don't think most European riders had ever seen a jumper turned out that way, with really perfect braiding and ears and whiskers trimmed. No doubt it looked like a lot of extra trouble to them back then, but now almost everyone does it.

Chapter 12

~

Stable Management

~

Introduction:
Stable Management
and Horsemanship

There are riders and there are horsemen. A rider is a person who can ride horses, perhaps a little or perhaps very well. A horseman is one who not only rides (although some fine horsemen do not ride at all) but also seeks to *know* the horse—its nature, needs, and management— and feels a deep personal responsibility for his horses, the care they get, and the life they lead. A rider may receive his horse already tacked up at the mounting block and turn it back to the groom when he is finished with it. The horseman has a vital interest in and deep knowledge of every aspect of his horse's care and well-being, whether or not he personally performs each necessary task. While anyone with the physical skills, the determination, and the money or opportunity to ride may become a good rider, to become a horseman is the work of a lifetime. The process of becoming a horseman requires three things:

long-term practical experience with many horses; lifetime learning in the ways, care, and handling of horses; and the development of a deep commitment to horses and a "horsemanlike" attitude. None of these can be bought, acquired overnight, or conferred like a degree.

We in North America are lucky to have had a long tradition of taking care of our horses ourselves. From the farmer to the cowboy, through the development of our horsemanship from its U.S. cavalry roots to the hunting field and show ring, our riders have been expected and taught to groom and tack their own horses, to cool them out, to help with veterinary and farrier care, and often to take full care of their horses themselves. There is less social prejudice against doing hands-on work for one's own horse in the United States than is present in some other countries and cultures. Here such work is not regarded as menial or beneath one's dignity, but as a necessary part of horsemanship and one of the rewarding sides of the human-animal relationship.

This attitude has made it easier for young people to acquire one of the essentials for becoming a horseman: namely, practical experience in horse care and handling. Our educational youth organizations, the U.S. Pony Clubs and the 4-H Horse Clubs, provide good sound basics in horse care and management to children and new horse owners, and most conscientious riding teachers try to give at least some basic instruction in grooming, tacking, basic horse care, and handling. This contact with horses has several benefits for riders of any age: it teaches essential horsemanship knowledge, without which horses cannot be kept sound and healthy; it teaches confidence and competence in working with horses; and finally, it helps the rider learn to love, respect, and relate to his horse as a living animal and a unique individual.

One of the most important aspects of the true horseman is his "horsemanlike" attitude, which is expressed in his thinking, in his conduct, and in the way he presents his horses, his facility, and himself. Perhaps the best word for this attitude is "respect": respect for the horse —*any* horse—as a living creature; respect for other people, in and out of the horse world; respect for those who have achieved stature as horsemen through their accomplishments; respect for tradition and hard work; respect for himself. A true horseman usually doesn't have a lot to say (unless he is in a teaching situation); he lets his actions and his results speak for him. Safety, competence, efficiency, and neatness are the marks of a good horseman, and everything he does has a reason for it, instead of being merely stylized or part of the latest fad. His horses' welfare comes before his own, and whatever he does with horses is based on his best understanding of horses' nature and needs, although he is humble enough to admit that he is still learning and will never know it all. The best way to learn to be a horseman is to watch, listen to, learn from, and emulate the best horsemen you can find.

Unfortunately, it is becoming harder today for young riders and new horse owners to get the practical experience in horse care and handling and the exposure to the old, traditional horseman's ways that former generations grew up with. Few today grow up on a horse farm or ranch, and fewer still are lucky enough to know an older horseman (or woman!) from whom they can learn as apprentice from master. Today's fast pace, lifestyle, and urban sprawl have limited many people to weekly lessons or to riding a horse that is boarded out and cared for by someone else. High costs and competitive pressure can lead some riders to narrow their focus to showing and honing their competitive skills, often to the exclusion of all else. An expensive, high-powered show horse requires competent professional handling, and sometimes owners are encouraged only to take their lessons, ride, show, and pay the bills and leave horse care and management decisions to the professionals. This unfortunate trend can lead to the development of superficial riders who know little about their horses and who sometimes have very little commitment to the animal, his welfare, or the lifetime satisfactions of real horsemanship.

Happily, there is in most riders a strong attraction for the animal, which is often the reason the rider took up riding instead of some other sport. It is the responsibility of instructors, coaches, trainers, and all real horsemen to nurture this interest and to provide education and leadership in developing their students and clients as *horsemen*, not just as riders or customers.

The Team and Organization

The care and management of a competition horse is as important as his riding and training, although it requires different skills and knowledge. Few people are such accomplished all-around horsemen that they can ride, teach, train, manage, and care for horses equally well. Even if one has the knowledge, it is virtually impossible to do all these jobs adequately under the time constraints of showing even one horse. Hence, the rider, trainer or coach, stable manager, and groom are all important members of the same team with a common goal: to get horse and rider to the ring on four good legs, physically and mentally ready to do their best. (Two other indispensable members of the team are a good farrier and an equine veterinarian.)

Each team member must respect the expertise and contributions of the others and must be willing to listen, to communicate, and to get the "big picture" by considering the input of the others, not just his own viewpoint. The groom cannot ride or train the horse, nor can the rider always see the details of the horse's well-being in the way that the groom can; neither can orchestrate the smooth functioning of the stable at home and on the road as can a good stable manager. It behooves each member of the team to do his own job as well as possible and to cooperate with the others, keeping the common goal of the horse's welfare and success foremost in mind. There must be a captain or a final authority for every team; in most cases, this is the stable manager in the area of horse care, and the trainer—or owner and trainer together—as the ultimate authority.

Good management requires organization, attention to details, and good communication. The rider and trainer will discuss the horse's program, goals, and schedule with the stable manager; the groom, through the stable manager, must report small changes that can be significant, such as a filled leg, a mishap during turnout, or a horse going off his feed. The horse's attitude and behavior during schooling and competition may point to the need for a change in feeding, exercise, or management. This should be discussed with the stable manager so that he can accommodate the needs of the horse, rider, and trainer and make informed decisions about horse care and management details. The rider and trainer can make better training decisions and can often prevent small problems from developing into real trouble if they receive timely information about the horse's physical state, appearance, and attitude in the stable.

The way a horse is handled in his stable routine can have a significant effect on his attitude and behavior in training and competition. Many of our show horses are hot, sensitive Thoroughbreds or near-Thoroughbreds; some have difficult temperaments or ground manners (behavior when not mounted) as a legacy of the race track or simply by nature. The groom (or anyone else who handles the horse) has a heavy responsibility for the horse's safety as well as his own. Sloppiness, lack of awareness, temper, or lack of self-discipline can lead to dangerous incidents, especially with high-strung and highly conditioned horses, young horses, and stallions. You cannot trust a horse to think or act like a human, but you can always expect him to act like a horse! Handlers must be able to anticipate problems and take steps to prevent them before they happen—like removing the wheelbarrow from the aisleway before leading a headstrong colt through. When a horse must be corrected, it should be prompt, brief, and effective, and it must be accomplished without provoking a reaction that could cause the horse to injure himself or someone else. There are times when a horse must be reprimanded or shown clearly where the limits are, but yelling, slapping, jerking, and shanking are the marks of a butcher, not a horseman, on the ground as well as in the saddle.

Each horse is a unique individual with his own special needs. The best grooms and stable managers learn their horses' likes and dislikes, and by meeting the animals' mental as well as their physical needs, they keep their horses happy, relaxed, and in the best frame of mind in which to be trained or shown. This may require tailoring exercise or turnout to a horse's liking; hand walking or grazing him early on the day of a competition; tempting his appetite with the foods he likes best; or perhaps omitting procedures that cause him to become excited or upset before a competition, such as braiding for certain horses. A horse that is intelligently and sympathetically handled in his stable care and routine comes to training with a better learning attitude and ability to cope with stress than one that is confused, frustrated, or frightened by his ground handlers.

Good organization makes everyone's job less hectic and promotes communication between rider, trainer, groom, and stable manager. A daily barn log that lists work schedules, turnout or other exercise, medications and/or bandages or other treatments, and special notes for each horse makes it easier to know what has been going on, and sometimes to identify a problem or find a solution. A daily work list is posted, detailing general barn duties, tasks to be done for each horse, and who is responsible for doing them. Don't rely on memory, verbal orders, or "usual routine"—write it down and check it off! When the farrier or veterinarian comes, he should have a list of horses to see with written notes on each horse. Following the visit, shoeing notes, veterinary diagnoses, treatments, and orders should be recorded in the log.

Each horse will have a permanent file containing documents (or photocopies) such as registration papers, insurance documents, health certificate, Coggins tests, AHSA registration number, and FEI passport (for horses competing in Grand Prix or under FEI rules). Up-to-date records of inoculations, deworming, blood tests, X rays, shoeing, and any veterinary treatments and medications should be kept there, too. The horse's vital signs (resting pulse, temperature, and respiration rate) should be recorded; this information is often kept on the stall card. A smaller file containing photocopies of documents required by shows (such as Coggins tests, AHSA number, vaccination certificates, and the like) should be prepared to travel with the horse to shows.

The Facility

The first impression one gets on entering a stable or equestrian facility is often a true one. The facility is the environment in which the major work of riding, training, and horse care is done at home, and the way it is set up and kept says a lot about the competence and horsemanship of the people in charge. A facility need not be elaborate to be excellent; a simple, workmanlike facility that is well organized and intelligently managed provides a better working environment than a lavishly decorated showplace that puts more emphasis on window dressing than on function.

Because of the wide range of climate, land, and rural, suburban, and urban settings for North American horse facilities, there are many different types of facilities and approaches to horse management. The horseman may have to cope with heat and humidity in the Deep South, winds and dust in the West, cold winters in the North, and other environmental factors. Some horsemen are located far from services, horse shows, and even neighbors; others must operate on a tiny plot hemmed in by urban sprawl. Feed, forage, and natural footing also vary widely with location. This makes it impossible to set a narrow definition of "correct" American stable management; instead we must focus on the basic principles that apply in any environment. It is possible to achieve an excellent horse care and training environment in a variety of facilities—from the traditional horse farm, sprawling ranch, or modern equestrian center to a backyard stable and paddock.

The first requisite in any horse facility is that it be designed for *horses*. The more we know about horses when setting up a facility, the stronger and safer we will build it. Horsemen know better than to use flimsy materials for stall construction, wire for fencing, or chewable soft wood for stalls and paddocks, or to skimp on stall size or the width of aisles and doorways. Horsemen know that horses spook, that they kick walls and fight over fences, and that if a horse can find a way to get hurt, he will. Horsemen design their stalls, aisles, doorways, gates, and paddocks with horse nature in mind. A perimeter fence with a gate barring access to the roadway can prevent an accidental escape from becoming a tragedy. Projections, sharp corners, gaps, and similar traps are eliminated from stables, aisleways, and paddocks. Consideration should be given to traffic patterns—for pedestrians and the public, led horses, mounted riders, and vehicular traffic.

Two notable characteristics of good facilities are simplicity and neatness. Simplicity comes from an absence of clutter in the design and setup; it requires thought about where things should go for safety, neatness, and efficiency. Neatness is the day-to-day cleanliness that comes from keeping things tidy, put away in their proper places, and in good repair. A neat facility is safer for people and horses and is more efficient to work in than an untidy, unorganized barn. Simplicity and neatness are functional and elegant; they have nothing to do with needless busywork or fussiness.

Efficiency is the hallmark of any well-run operation. Efficiency means making the most intelligent use of available facilities and resources, including time, to do the job without wasted time or effort. Inefficient design and methods are wasteful of time and labor, which are particularly expensive in this country. (An example of inefficient design is a facility designed so that horses have to be led half a mile to the turnout paddocks, or one that requires stall cleaners to negotiate a maze of narrow aisles to push a wheelbarrow to the manure pit.) If it is unnecessarily difficult and time-consuming to get through the ordinary daily work, the staff becomes frustrated, harried, and slipshod, and horse care soon suffers. It also becomes nearly impossible to keep good staff.

No facility can remain in good working order without constant maintenance. Horses and people are hard on their environment; minor breakage and wear and tear are constant factors. It is all too easy to let small problems go indefinitely until the whole facility has deteriorated and a major overhaul is required. In order for staff to keep a facility in working order, proper tools and materials must be available, and someone must be responsible for maintenance and repairs. This must be given a high enough priority that it is not put off until "somebody" has time.

One of the most important considerations for the jumping sports is footing. Nothing matters more to the safety and confidence of horse and rider and the long-term soundness of the horse. While at a show, a competitor must cope with whatever conditions come up; at home he must be able to work his horses consistently on safe footing regardless of the weather. Footing for jumping must be secure, prevent slipping, and be somewhat resilient but not too deep. It cannot have hard spots, deep places, or slick spots, and it must not become unusable because of rain, dust, mud, or freezing. Natural turf is an ideal surface for galloping and jumping, but it requires careful maintenance and is easily damaged. Dirt, sand, loam, and fiber surfaces require good drainage, dust control, watering, and harrowing or dragging to keep them even and in good condition. Indoor arenas are apt to develop uneven depth of footing and hard spots along the track if they are not dragged and leveled regularly.

Finally, a facility for jumping needs jumps. While it is certainly advantageous to have a full range of show jumping equipment, a good trainer can create the variety he needs by repositioning, recombining, and sometimes repainting the simple elements that make up obstacles and courses. Whether his jumps are homemade or designed for a Grand Prix, they must be sturdy, safely constructed, and well maintained. Flimsy jumps, light rails, and shallow cups teach horses that it is just as easy to knock down a jump as to jump it properly, and this can eventually lead to sloppy jumping and even accidents. No part of a standard or obstacle should be capable of trapping a horse if he should slide into it; extra cups should be removed from standards when not in use (but not dumped on the ground!), and unused equipment should be stored neatly outside the ring. Natural obstacles such as banks, ditches, and water jumps are invaluable in developing bold, free, and natural jumpers, but they must be properly designed and constructed in order to be safe. *Designing Courses and Obstacles* (Pamela Carruthers, George H. Morris, et al.) contains good information on jump construction and setting appropriate courses for schooling and competition. One essential for jumping is a ground person (or crew) who can adjust fences as needed. Courses should be changed regularly (weekly if possible) for training purposes, to allow for maintenance of the footing, and to avoid damaging the turf.

Evaluation of a New Horse

When a new horse arrives at the stable, whether a young prospect or a currently campaigning show horse, he will be evaluated for fitness and general health and condition. While one might expect that an expensive horse or one from a well-known stable would be in top condition, experience has shown that this is not always the case. The evaluation process is easier if complete records on the horse's inoculations, veterinary work, deworming, shoeing, and general care are available.

The first step is a thorough veterinary examination, noting vital signs and examining the various systems, feet, and legs. A blood count will be run and, if normal, will serve as a baseline against which future tests may be compared. If the horse was recently purchased, he may have had current X rays of the feet and joints as part of the prepurchase exam. Some managers have X rays taken every year or six months in order to spot developing problems before they lead to actual lameness. The teeth will be checked by an equine dental specialist for sharp edges, wolf teeth, and dental abnormalities, and they will be floated if necessary.

The horse's shoeing, way of moving, and general level of fitness are also evaluated. When a mature horse is in steady work and going well, it may be more prudent to keep on shoeing him in the way he has been shod than to experiment too much in the hope of improving him. If he has problems that will require shoeing changes, these will usually be made gradually in order to avoid overstressing the tendons, ligaments, and structures of the feet and joints by too radical a change all at once.

If current information is not available on the horse's previous inoculations or deworming program, he will be dewormed and started on an immunization program. Young horses that have spent most of their life on the farm are especially susceptible to virus infections when they encounter a "bug" that they have never been exposed to before; ideally, they should have been inoculated long enough before shipping to boost their immunity before exposure to a new population of horses. It is prudent to isolate a new horse for ten days to two weeks on arrival.

Deworming and Health Care

No horse can respond to a conditioning program if he is infested with internal parasites, and all horses are exposed to these parasites in the course of their daily lives. In addition, the damage caused to blood vessels and internal organs by parasites is a major cause of colic and can lead to fatalities. All good stable managers practice a continuing parasite control program, including deworming every six to eight weeks or on a schedule recommended by the veterinarian.

Cleanliness and good management are just as important as regular deworming in parasite control. The most damaging parasites are ingested as eggs when horses eat grass or feed that has been contaminated by manure, particularly in overgrazed paddocks. Picking up manure from paddocks, good stall cleaning, keeping feed clean and off the ground, and frequent dragging, mowing, and rotating of pastures are important management practices for controlling parasites.

Since show horses are exposed to large numbers of horses that may carry communicable diseases while their resistance is lowered by the stress of shipping and competing, they require more attention with regard to immunization than the horse that never leaves home. A carefully followed immunization program will keep the horse's immune system ready to fight off most infectious diseases; such a program may at least allow the horse to escape with a lighter case if he does pick up a "bug."

The veterinarian will advise which diseases to inoculate against, which products to use, and how often booster shots are necessary. The required inoculations must be done long enough before shipping or competition to ensure that the horse's immunity will be high. Inoculations, like deworming, can cause the horse some stress or a mild reaction and can give him a couple of "off" days. They should be scheduled on the calendar and planned so as not to interfere with shipping, showing, or a major schooling session.

Most show stables have a blood count done on each horse every three months to check for anemia. This test would also be run if a horse is lethargic, underweight, or not responding to a conditioning program.

The horse's dental condition should be checked twice a year by an equine dental specialist. Sharp edges on the teeth, abnormal jaw or tooth formation, retained baby teeth, or wolf teeth can cause mouth pain, head tossing, and resistance to the bit that cannot be trained away. Floating the teeth can give the horse relief from pain and help him chew and digest his feed more efficiently, making a significant difference in his condition and often in his disposition as well. Young horses shedding baby teeth, old horses, and those with mouth abnormalities may need attention more often.

Daily Care

Good managers know that meticulous care, day in and day out, matters most in bringing a horse to the ring fit to show. Attention to details without losing sight of the goals and the overall picture is the hallmark of the top-flight stable and horseman. A well-conceived daily routine ensures that each horse gets the feeding, turnout, stall care, grooming, and other attentions he needs. Intelligent application of that routine meets special individual needs.

American horsemen believe in turnout, and intelligent use of turnout and pasture time can be indispensable in managing horses. Turnout and grazing are good for the horse's physical and mental condition; they promote relaxation, good digestion, and natural exercise. Most horses are turned out for at least a short period daily while at home, and some individuals do better when turned out all day or all night when space, climate, and insect problems permit. Valuable horses should be protected from accidental injuries during turnout by bell boots, polo wraps, and/or front and hind leg boots, and the turnout paddock must be safely fenced and have good footing.

Because a horse spends so many hours in his stall, it is essential that the stall provide a clean, safe, and comfortable environment. The stall must be large enough for comfort and to avoid the horse getting cast; it must also be free from projections or other hazards that could injure a horse or trap a leg or his head. Ventilation and freedom from drafts are especially important for the horse's health; constant exposure to dust from an adjoining indoor arena can lead to chronic respiratory troubles. The type of bedding used is a matter of individual choice, but stalls must be bedded deeply enough to encourage the horse to lie down and rest and to prevent stress on the feet and legs. Stalls will be thoroughly cleaned daily and picked out frequently in any well-run stable.

Daily grooming is as important for health and conditioning reasons as it is for the horse's appearance. During grooming, the groom does a careful hands-on check of the horse's condition, which will often catch small problems before they can escalate into larger ones.

The skin and hair coat are essential in regulating the horse's temperature and sweating mechanism during work. Excessive dirt, grease, and scurf on the skin result in thick, gummy lather which does not evaporate easily and stresses the horse by overheating him during work; this lather can also cause sores, irritation, and skin infections where the skin is rubbed by the tack. Thorough daily grooming clears the skin and hair coat for more efficient elimination of waste products; it also makes the horse look better, and only conscientious daily grooming and rubbing will produce a "show glow."

A horse should always be brushed over and have his feet picked out, his legs checked, his mane and tail brushed free from bedding and debris, and any mud or manure stains removed before he is ridden, even if only for schooling or exercise. Likewise, he should always be put away cool, clean, and comfortable after work, whether he is bathed, toweled off, or brushed over. The thorough grooming that conditions the coat and skin is most effective after exercise, when the skin is warm and the pores are open. Bathing after exercise and special grooming before a show are part of the process, but they are no substitutes for meticulous daily care.

Close attention to the condition and soundness of the legs is of paramount importance in the care of the jumping horse. Many older campaigners have old injuries, scar tissue, or chronic conditions that must be properly cared for to keep these horses working sound. Good leg care starts with a close daily inspection by the groom, a habit that the rider and trainer should also emulate. Any minor changes or abnormalities, such as filling or heat, should be noticed, investigated, and treated immediately, and the horse's work, exercise, or competition schedule may have to be adjusted.

Hand rubbing or massage of the legs can be very helpful, especially when dealing with an older horse, one with chronic leg problems, or one with stiffness and filling. Other therapies, such as hydromassage or whirlpool treatment, ultrasound, electrical stimulation, and cold laser therapy, should be used only by those trained in their proper application, preferably with advice from the veterinarian.

To bandage or not to bandage is an individual decision which depends on the needs of the horse and the judgment of his caretakers. Since horses do become dependent upon bandages if they are constantly wrapped, some managers prefer not to wrap unless it is necessary for shipping, support after work, or treatment of an injury. Others prefer to use standing bandages as a routine precaution, especially when the horse is stabled in temporary stabling at a show where the chances of stall injuries are greater than at home. Horses that have a weakness or old injury may require regular bandaging, massage, and other therapy just to keep them working sound. Certainly any bandages must be expertly applied and must be checked frequently; they should be removed and reset twice a day.

Medications are part of the reality of managing competition horses today. While it is self-defeating not to take advantage of advances in veterinary treatment that can help a horse work in comfort and extend his competitive career, a good horseman will keep legal and ethical considerations and the horse's long-term welfare in mind. There is a difference between medication as legitimate therapy and medication in order to mask a problem for the short term. The first is intended to help the horse heal or at least to allow him to be comfortable; the second puts the horse's future soundness at risk.

When the horse is competing, medication enters the province of the American Horse Shows Association and/or the FEI. The rules governing medications permitted in competition are specific, the penalties for violation are tough, and the trend is toward ever tighter regulation. No horseman can afford to be ignorant of the medication rules—especially of seemingly innocuous substances that may contain forbidden ingredients, or of how long a forbidden substance may remain in the horse's system. A conservative approach to medication, along with sound veterinary advice and knowledge of the rules, is the safest policy for horsemen and their horses.

Feeding, Weight, and Condition

We must realize to what extent we are working against nature in feeding and managing competition horses. Horses have evolved for fifty million years as grazers; their systems are equipped to handle constant grazing, plenty of roughage, and free exercise. When we confine a horse to a stall for twenty-three hours a day, do short periods of intense work, limit his hay to keep his belly slim, and feed him large amounts of highly concentrated grain, we are asking him to adapt to an unnatural lifestyle. Sometimes it isn't successful. The closer horses can be kept to the way nature intended, the fewer digestive, metabolic, and behavior problems we are likely to see. Unfortunately, we must often adjust our feeding and management to the realities of large stables, limited pasture time, and the pressures of competition and the show circuit. Within this context, careful feeding—and balancing the feed and exercise to meet the individual horse's needs—can reduce stress on horses and help each horse get the best out of his feeding and conditioning program.

Good managers make sure each horse is fed a ration that is nutritionally balanced. The ration must meet the horse's basic requirements in energy (calories), protein, vitamins, minerals, and roughage. Balancing a ration requires some information about the components of the feed (such information can be obtained from the ingredients tag or by having the feed analyzed), some nutritional charts, and a little math.

Once the computations are done, the manager can be sure that the feed meets his horses' basic nutritional requirements without deficiencies, waste, or dangerous excesses, and the basic feed can be adjusted in makeup and quantity to meet the needs of each individual horse.

Other good feeding practices include attention to cleanliness, top-quality feed, a regular feeding schedule, and adjusting each horse's daily feed according to his condition, work, and temperament. The hay, grain, and other feed must be of the best quality, as spoiled grain or dusty hay can cause serious digestive and respiratory problems. Each horse must be fed and treated as an individual, and his needs will vary from day to day. A horse that goes off his feed or drinks more or less than usual may be reacting to weather, stress, or distractions, or he may be developing an illness; it is important that the person who feeds knows his horses well enough to notice and follow up on such signs.

The object of a feeding and conditioning program is to bring the horse into the best physical condition for that individual, considering the job he has to do. American show horses are expected to look sleek and attractive, and a noticeably poor or underweight animal will cast aspersions on the person who rides and cares for him. Beyond this, there is a range of acceptable condition.

American show hunters, particularly Thoroughbreds, should be healthy but not excessively fit, or they may become temperamentally difficult. Conformation hunters especially are expected to be nicely rounded, in "big" condition. Of course, no jumping horse can afford to be unfit or obese to the point that his legs, feet, and structure are stressed by the weight he carries, or he will quickly become unsound. He should not huff and puff during the normal work of a lesson, a course, or an under-saddle class. Many Thoroughbreds do better on good-quality hay, complete feed pellets, or a feed containing beet pulp for fiber than when fed excessive amounts of hard feed. Overgraining a horse to make him fat and sassy and then longeing him into the ground to make him rideable is more apt to produce a cripple than a winner, but it is an all too common mistake.

Jumpers need to be fitter than show hunters and require more energy-producing feed for the physical demands of their work. A jumper should not be fed so much grain that he gets above himself, but he must be more aerobically fit than the show hunter for the demands of schooling, competing over a long course, and jumping against the clock. Jumpers are usually fed more concentrated feed and usually do more fitness work. However, the individual horse's type and temperament must be taken into account. Some horses, especially warmbloods, easily become overweight and need to be kept quite fit; they may need more grain, more work, and less hay. A more "nervy" Thoroughbred type may burn off more energy and keep himself fit if not thin; he may need to relax as much as he can, and plenty of hay and turnout may help keep him in reasonable weight as well as keeping him contented.

Children's horses and amateurs' horses often need to be quiet, sensible, and amenable to ride, yet they must look like show horses. They are sometimes worked harder than other horses if the rider is taking lessons, practicing a lot, and showing heavily, too. The very placid and lazy horse will need to be fed more grain and gotten more fit than the "hyper" horse, who will be more levelheaded if he is not overgrained.

The rider must work with the trainer and stable manager in adhering to a sensible level of exercise for the horse. Failure to ride the horse consistently will result in an unfit horse who can be easily injured if he is then overworked in a burst of enthusiasm. Turnout and longeing are fine in their place, but they are no substitute for regular riding. Riders who take vacations or have hectic schedules must make arrangements to have their horses ridden when they cannot, or they must accept the consequences by limiting their activities to what their unfit horses can safely handle. On the other hand, serious competitive riders sometimes forget that their horses (and they themselves) can benefit from some quiet, undemanding hacking or trail riding as a refresher and a break from constant drilling.

Foot Care and Shoeing

With the stress that jumping puts on the horse's feet and legs, surely nothing is more important than good foot care and shoeing. Good daily care is not difficult, but it requires meticulous attention to picking out the feet and watching the condition of the frog, sole, wall, and shoes. Hoof dressing may be used to keep the heels and coronary band flexible, but a buildup of sticky dressing on the hoof wall does nothing to moisturize the foot and is unnecessarily messy. For competition, most American hunter and jumper exhibitors prefer a light oil hoof dressing instead of hoof polish, which has an artificially painted look and must be removed after showing.

The hoof is moisturized and kept flexible by its own internal circulation (which is stimulated by the pumping action of the frog as the horse exercises) and by absorbing moisture through the coronary band and the ground surface of the foot. The ground conditions and the surface on which the horse stands have much to do with the condition of the feet. Excessively hard, dry ground conditions can lead to dry, hard, and contracted feet; working in abrasive sand can wear away the protective outer covering of the hoof wall; and constant exposure to wet, swampy conditions can cause the feet to absorb so much moisture that they become too soft and break off easily. Dry, bruised, or sensitive feet may be packed overnight with prepared clay, which alleviates the dryness, making the feet more flexible and less apt to sting on impact with the ground. Hoof sealants may be used on horses who have abraded feet, whose feet crack badly, and who have difficulty in holding a shoe.

In shoeing, as in bitting, the best rule is "Whatever works!" Each individual horse must be shod with the hoof angle and type of shoes that allow him to be comfortable and move his best, with the least possible stress on his feet and legs. While the ideal horse should stand and move perfectly straight without winging in or paddling, too radical efforts to "correct" the horse's way of moving or standing can force the structures of the foot and leg out of alignment and sometimes can cause more harm than the original defect. Corrective shoeing is more necessary for horses with functional gait problems, such as interfering, overreaching, or forging, than for cosmetic purposes.

The angle of the hoof is critical to the horse's comfort and soundness. The hoof should be trimmed and balanced so that the angle of the foot matches the angle of the pastern and the hoof lands in a natural balance without twisting or rocking. Excessive lowering of the heels in an effort to lengthen the stride puts stress on the deep flexor tendon and the navicular bone and may contribute to early breakdowns. Some horses require special support in the form of a bar shoe, an egg bar shoe, degree pads, or other special shoes. While these indicate a weakness and hence may be penalized in hunter classes, there is no choice if they are necessary for the horse's working soundness.

Hunters are judged on their long, low movement; hence their shoes should be no heavier than necessary. Many wear aluminum plates. A jumper's feet are subjected to more stress than a hunter's feet when jumping, landing, and turning; his shoes may need to be more substantial so that they will not easily bend or twist under the strain. Traction devices like rim shoes, calks, and screw-in studs give the horse stability and confidence when jumping, turning, and galloping on certain surfaces. For competition, jumpers often wear shoes that are tapped for screw-in studs so that the right studs for the ground conditions can be inserted before a class. Horses that fold their forelegs tightly under their chest may need to wear a leather chest protector to protect against self-inflicted injuries from studs when jumping, and bell boots are often used for protection when the horse wears studs. Studs should be removed immediately after a class, as a horse can injure himself if he strikes himself or steps on his coronary band while wearing them.

A Jumping Turn
Tim Grubb displays some classic dressage elements while turning on course. His eyes are looking at his next fence; his hip angle has opened, deepening his seat and helping him retain good posture. His inside leg is down by the girth with the heel down, while his outside leg has gone about a hand's width behind the girth, also with the heel down. The horse is bent around his inside leg from head to tail. While this is not a particularly pleasant picture of the horse, it is one of very good riding.

Coming out of a Turn
Grubb is an Englishman who has always ridden the American Jumping Style. Notice the classic American leg! Especially for turning and jumping, the leg must be in contact with the horse, and the seat deep in the saddle. One has the distinct feeling that Grubb not only is allowing this horse to come forward out of this turn, but is even driving him on in what is probably a time class or a jump-off.

The Horse's Head and Neck
Contrary to popular belief, horses extend and even raise their head and neck while galloping and jumping in their natural state. Why do we riders spend so much time tying them down? Ego and control, I suspect. Let a horse be a horse! Grubb is showing us a correct position galloping toward a fence, and how the four parts of the rider's body (leg, base of support, upper body, and hands and arms) should work. I especially like the straight line from the rider's elbow to the horse's mouth, which is only marred by a slightly too short running martingale.

A Broken Line Above the Mouth A broken line above the mouth is acceptable, and it is often preferable to a broken line below the horse's mouth. It is used especially on low, heavy-headed horses and on stoppers. Eric Hasbrouck, who is in a classic position, is demonstrating this broken line perfectly. Preferred by the French, who have lots of low-headed horses, and North Americans who ride Thoroughbreds, this technique of "high hands" is usually frowned upon by those of the continental schools.

The American Jumping Style Here is a picture of the American Jumping Style—every detail is there. The stirrup is on the ball of the foot with the outside branch touching the little toe. The heels are down and in, with the ankles flexed and the toes out fifteen to forty-five degrees. The calf of the leg is in contact with the horse, while the base of support (seat and thighs) is deep in the saddle. The eyes are up and ahead, and the upper body is inclined forward up to thirty degrees. There is a perfectly straight line from the rider's elbow to the horse's mouth. Hasbrouck and his horse, both conditioned athletes, are beautifully turned out. They truly represent the American Jumping Style.

Dressage While Jumping

Matz is not only one of the greatest classicists of all time in jumping a fence, but also a master at riding on the flat. Here he is turning between fences. The horse is uniformly bent around the rider's inside leg and hand. His hocks are under him, and his head and neck couldn't be better placed. Matz and his horse are both looking in the direction of movement.

An Aggressive Ride

Matz is not just a stylist; as shown here, he is also an aggressive rider who can attack a jump-off with the best. Notice how the rider's body functions under the pressure of a "time turn." The toes come out and the heels down and in; the seat drops down and back to drive. The upper body opens up but remains in front of the vertical, with the eyes always up and looking in the direction of movement. The hands and arms stay soft and giving, allowing the horse to go forward. Notice the horse's balance: the head and shoulders are elevated and light; most of the weight is carried on the hindquarters, with the hocks well engaged.

Self-carriage

A well-balanced horse carries himself as shown here. This horse is carrying himself and his rider. Matz is able, in this situation, to sit on the horse's back, use his legs, and keep a light, fine contact with the mouth. The horse accepts the aids and appreciates their support. Matz is "behind the motion" of his horse; this maximizes his ability to drive.

A Racing Seat

It is evident, from looking through these photos how many different upper body positions we use when jumping a course. Racing through the finish line, we use a racing seat. Mary Ann Steiert is "ahead of the motion" for this purpose, getting up off her horse's back, relieving the hindquarters, and putting her weight forward over her horse's shoulders. While this is the best position for the racing gallop, it is not at all advantageous for jumping or turning.

The Indirect Rein

The French invented it all, and they are still showing us. Durand is making a turn on course while giving us a perfect demonstration of the indirect rein (rein of opposition) in front of the withers. Notice the line from the left side of the horse's mouth toward Durand's right hip. This rein aid displaces the horse's weight from shoulder to shoulder, as well as bending him in his head and neck.

Heels Down!

The degree to which one is able to get his heels down depends on his conformation. Durand apparently has very flexible ankles, which provide him with great security and a viselike grip. His crotch is in the saddle more than his buttocks on this shallow turn, making his seat lighter. His upper body is in a correct galloping position—approximately thirty degrees in front of the vertical, with an impeccably straight back and hollowed-out loins—and his eyes are up. On this "overbent" horse, a broken line above the mouth is appropriate.

Absorbing the Shock

Blaton is absorbing the shock of landing over this big oxer in her ankle, knee, and hip joints. With her heels driven down, most of the shock is absorbed in her ankle joints. The same is true of her horse. Notice how the horse's fetlock is almost touching the ground. Obviously there is tremendous wear and tear on horses' joints during galloping and jumping.

Long Release—European Style

Fuchs has apparently adopted the American long crest release with much success. His horse seems to enjoy the freedom—his ears and eyes are alert, head and neck stretched out and down, knees up, and back very round. He is giving this fence at least a foot. Techniques such as the long release, frowned upon by Europeans ten years ago, are now gladly accepted and practiced.

An Irishman and the American Jumping Style

Mullins, an Irishman, has admittedly learned from our North American ways. His stirrup is on the ball of his foot; his leg is in a perfect position, with the stirrup leather perpendicular to the ground. His seat (crotch and buttocks) is deep in the saddle, with his upper body inclined forward and his eyes up. There is an absolutely straight line from elbow to horse's mouth, *not* broken by a too short running martingale. The horse is allowed to carry his forehand "up," enabling him to balance himself with head and neck.

Elegance in Motion   The American Jumping Style inherited much of its elegance from the French. Here Frederic Cottier is all elegance while making a very short approach to a very tall gate. His position for galloping and jumping could not be improved on. This is style! Analyze every part of this rider's body—all is correct.

Just Before Takeoff   The legs close with the heels down; the seat deepens; the upper body remains inclined forward "with" the horse; the arms and hands yield. The horse is balanced, encouraged, and allowed. What more can be done?

Taking Off The legs are "there" with the heels down and the toes slightly out. The horse's thrust throws the seat forward and up out of the saddle along with the upper body. The eyes do not drop but remain up and ahead. The hands release the mouth—though in this instance, at a big vertical, they do not lose light contact. Again, the rider's style could not be improved on.

During Flight Cottier again exhibits style and elegance in action. Unfortunately he has "lost" his leg a bit in the air; it has slipped up and back. As I have said before, this habit is more often seen in Europe than in North America. I love the generosity and sensitivity of his hands and upper body, which in no way interfere with the horse's jump.

On the Descent Cottier is coming back into the saddle and onto his horse's mouth gradually and with feeling. He has no intention of "stiffing" the horse in the air by mistake.

The Landing Coming down from a fence is so important. A horse must learn not to be defensive about his rider on landing. The shock is taken up primarily in the rider's ankles; he sinks down into the saddle rather than sitting down harshly or abruptly. He opens his hip angle and straightens up, slowly taking up a slightly stronger contact with the horse's mouth to regain control.

The German Style

Thomas Fruehmann, though Austrian, is one of the best examples of today's German School. This style, characterized by very long reins and a very deep seat, was made popular during the fifties by Alwin Schockemohle and Fritz Thiedemann, two of the biggest winners of that era. Though not a picturesque way of riding, this very long rein, deep seat, and erect upper body does work well with the colder, heavier German horse.

Landing like a Feather

Although David Broome is a big man today, his touch is nevertheless as soft as ever. Notice the lightness of his hands, arms, upper body, and seat as he lands here. He has always been a generous and giving rider to his horses, the highest compliment I can pay a fellow horseman.

The Long Release—With Mane

Although an elementary technique, grabbing mane is something we should all know how to do. Here Broome—one of the greatest jumping riders, if not *the* greatest—is showing us our own long release with mane, something I teach all beginners. He is not too proud to grab the mane instead of perhaps his horse's mouth. This is a good technique to fall back on whenever there is a chance of hitting the horse in the mouth.

Course Walking

It is better, when walking courses nowadays, to know too much than too little; one can always discard information, but the tiniest detail regarding fences, lines, and turns left to chance will surely lose a class. Here I am coaching the Swiss team at a European Championship. Most horsemen truly like to help each other. I have never found any national boundaries when it came to horses and sport. And we all certainly speak the same language.

The Facility

The stable, whether at home or at a show, reflects the style of horsemanship. Neatness and cleanliness have always been a part of the American ethic, especially when it comes to stable management.

Organization

Without perfect organization, there is nothing. People tend to forget things, so we write lists for everything.

Tack Room

Tack rooms on the road must house everything, not only tack. Space is at a premium. Here you see an office, bedroom, and tack room combined. This example of good housekeeping is the norm, not the exception. There is even a made-up bed for a nap or for the person on night duty.

Equipment

Equipment for horse and rider is very costly, but failing to maintain equipment properly is even more expensive, as well as dangerous and unacceptable. It takes work to maintain anything after it is purchased. Fundamental to style is that everything is kept scrupulously clean and in perfect repair.

Tack and Stable Supplies

"A place for everything and everything in its place." Here you see a supply cabinet, fly spray, a bandage and brush rack made from a milk container, a portable bridle rack, and a blanket rack. Everything is perfectly in order and scrupulously clean, with the bridles hung in "figure eight" fashion. Cleanliness and order are basic to style; they also are indicative of discipline.

Tack Trunk

Tack trunks should be packed in the same way every time, so items will always be in the same place. Trunks should be thoroughly cleaned out after every show, with each item individually cleaned and/or repaired and meticulously repacked. Notice the neat packing—the scrim sheet is neatly folded, the overgirth rolled, and the straps on the boots buckled. The white container holds the calks. Tack trunks need to be repainted frequently because of the wear and tear they get.

Space

Space is at a premium, both at home and at a show. Notice how efficiently the space in this small grooming stall has been used. Notice also that every single item has been cleaned before being put in its proper place. The stall has been raked and the cabinet polished.

The Stall

I do not like cinder block or stone stalls; they are hard on horses' hocks. However, on the road one must make do. The bedding has been "banked" high at the sides of the stall, which helps to prevent the horse from getting cast and may also protect his hocks somewhat. The stall should be thoroughly cleaned once a day and picked out many times during the day for the health and comfort of the horse and the cleanliness of the horse and his blankets.

Water Buckets

Rubber or plastic pails and feed tubs are easier on horses' hocks than metal ones, as pails and tubs are sure to get kicked. They should be hung at about the height of the point of the horse's shoulder (those in this photo look a bit low). Two water buckets ensure that the horse has fresh, clean water in front of him at all times. Buckets should be rinsed out and scoured with a stiff brush every day. Notice the flake of hay under the pail of water; horses should be able to dunk their hay in their water.

Feed Room

Here two stalls have been combined to make a feed room. Metal garbage cans are best, as they keep the feed clean and away from rodents. Hanging up rakes, shovels, brooms, and other tools on the wall in the feed room, not out in the aisles, is safer as well as neater.

Whirlpool

What a happy horse this is, standing in his whirlpool tub. Cool, circulating water, much like a cold stream, is nature's way of relieving inflammation, heat, swelling, and soreness. Ice or warm water can also be used in the whirlpool, depending on the problem. If we ask horses' legs to do more than they were meant to do, it is our job to look after their legs.

The Veterinarian

Dr. Danny Marks, DVM, a world-renowned veterinarian, has traveled with the American team's horses for years, and much of our success is owed to his expertise. He helps not only our horses, but anyone else's in need. Here he is palpating an ankle during a horse show. The veterinarian is probably the single most important person in a horse's support system.

Grooming

Good grooming means paying attention to the details and the out-of-the-way places as well as the obvious. Here, Jenny James, a woman from England, carries on our tradition of good grooming. Remember, the foundation of American horsemanship, and especially our stable management, is English. All English-speaking peoples like their animals and enjoy taking good care of them.

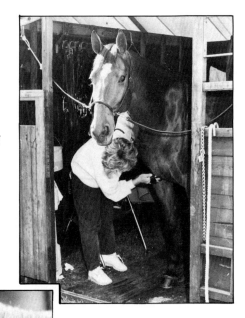

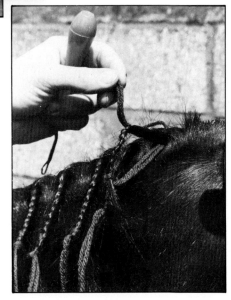

Mane Pulling

One sign of good grooming and presentation is a well-pulled mane. The mane should be kept short and even, just long enough for neat braiding. The length of the mane is approximately the width of one's hand. It should be pulled to an even length using a mane-pulling comb as shown here.

Braiding

Braiding the mane in the American way is beautiful and elegant. Nobody else does it quite the same; our style is a result of the turnout of our show hunters. The mane may be braided either with a needle and heavy thread or with yarn and a "pull-through" as shown here. All braids should be small, tight, and placed close together, flat against the neck. The yarn or thread should match the color of the mane or be of a conservative color, never a gaudy or bright color. Elastic bands are never used in braiding for a show.

Cleaning Tack

Here Jenny James, stable manager and groom, carries on the English tradition of meticulous tack care. By cleaning the leather daily with very little water and saddle soap, she keeps the leather supple and clean; she also checks for wear and needed repairs. Leather parts should be regularly disassembled and cleaned, and all metal parts cleaned and polished. Many classes have been lost through tack breaking while on course, usually a reflection of poor maintenance—and hence poor horsemanship.

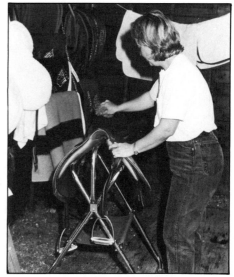

Cleaning a Shank

Style, especially the American Jumping Style, is a matter of detail. Here Jenny James is shown cleaning a chain lead shank. Notice the clean bridles hung in "figure eights," the polished metal, and the freshly laundered saddle pads and girth covers. Our "American look" is due to this attention to details and our "spit and polish" presentation.

Rolling Bandages

Bandages, the mainstay of horses' leg care, must be kept clean and properly rolled up, ready for use. Here José Padilla is doing it right, rolling the bandage tightly against his knee, with the (ultimately) outside end of the bandage rolled up in the center.

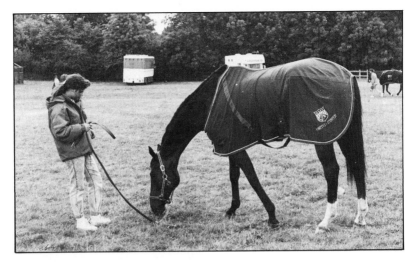

Grazing The American system of training centers around the horse being turned out in a paddock every day. Since this is usually impossible during a show, the next best thing is hand walking and grazing. Anything to get a horse out of his stall and get him to drop his head and relax in his natural state! What's wrong with this picture? First, the chain shank should be run through the halter ring and across the horse's nose for safer control in case he gets excited and tries to bolt. Secondly, sneakers are not really safe footwear for working around horses. They are too soft a shoe; toes can get broken!

The American Hunter So much of our American Jumping Style is a result of our upbringing on the American Thoroughbred-type hunter, both in terms of the presentation of horse and rider and in terms of our riding. Here is an example of a beautifully turned out show hunter—his condition, grooming, clip job, and braiding are all impeccable. We like our show jumpers to look the same. (It's too bad the woman is looking back at her horse as she jogs him out; she should look ahead instead.)

Chapter 13

~

*Horse Show
Presentation*

~

General

Horse shows are the showcase of the horse world—a public display of the talents of the horse and rider and of the work that has been done at home. They are an opportunity to measure one's horse, riding, training, and work against others. Going to a show unprepared is an exercise in futility and an embarrassment. By the same token, the stable management and presentation of the horse at a show demonstrate the standard of care and management practiced at home. A well-turned-out horse and rider make a good impression on the public and on potential new clients, while a sloppy or inappropriate presentation can repel prospective customers.

American horse shows have a long-standing tradition of high standards in turnout and presentation. Cleanliness, correct turnout, attention to details, and a certain polish are expected in all classes from beginner equitation to Grand Prix jumpers. While a clean saddle pad or a well-braided mane will not get you an extra six inches over an oxer, it does show that you know and care about the details. Sloppiness in presentation goes hand in hand with disorganization, ignorance, and lack of discipline in other areas (like riding and training). The top competitors get *all* the details right!

Cleanliness

The most basic requirement for show preparation is cleanliness— of the horse, the tack, the rider's turnout, and the stable area. A well-cared-for horse will be kept clean and in good condition to begin with; light-colored horses may need a bath before a show, and the tail and white markings will be shampooed. Silicone coat dressings applied to the coat and to white legs help to repel stains and dust for several days, but they should not be used on the saddle area, as they are slippery. Saddle pads, polo wraps, and other washable items should be freshly laundered, and spares taken to the show so that the horse need not appear in later classes with soiled or sweat-stained gear. The rider's clothes will be cleaned and pressed, with boots and spurs polished. Whenever the horse and rider appear in public, even during early morning schooling sessions, both should be clean and neat even in informal turnout. As tack and boots get dirty during schooling and warm-up, they will need a touch-up just before the rider goes into the ring; the horse will also get some last-minute attention. At the stable area, all equipment should be clean and in good repair when packed, and a good stable area will be tidy and well organized even if busy.

Clipping and Trimming

The look of the American Jumping Style is clean, sharp, and elegant. Good trimming of the horse's head, bridle path, and legs accentuates the clean lines of the Thoroughbred and can make even a plain horse look neat and trim. Poor trimming or excessive hair around the face and legs makes a horse look coarse and neglected.

The fetlocks and long hair of the legs are trimmed short with clippers—usually with the direction of the hair, so as not to clip too closely. All excess hair is trimmed from the jaw and muzzle, and the edges of the ears should be trimmed neatly. (It is not necessary to clip the insides of the ears clean; the hair can simply be trimmed neatly, which leaves some protection against insects.) A short bridle path (no more than an inch) may be clipped closely under the crownpiece of the bridle.

Horses showing during the winter may be body-clipped. While a hunter clip with the legs left unclipped is acceptable, this is more appropriate for horses that do not grow especially long hair. Trace clips and other partial clips should be reserved for field hunters and school horses—not for major shows. Thick-coated horses look better with a full clip; when they are reclipped, a hunter clip may do. Any clipping should be done neatly and thoroughly; nothing looks worse than a ragged, uneven clipping job.

Mane and Tail

American hunters and jumpers are traditionally shown with a short pulled mane, which is usually braided for shows. The tail may be free, braided, or put up in a mud knot.

The mane should be evenly pulled to a length of $3^1/2$ to $4^1/2$ inches. Smaller or more refined horses look best with shorter manes, which result in smaller braids; a slightly longer mane looks more in proportion on a massive horse. The mane must be pulled, not cut, to achieve a natural look and the right thickness for neat braiding.

Braiding calls attention to the top line of the neck and the way the horse uses his neck when working on the flat or over a fence. It also prevents a long, blowing mane from obscuring the line of the neck or getting tangled with the reins and stick. Braiding the mane is not a requirement, although it is traditional, especially for hunter and equitation classes and for formal occasions. Some horses, especially those with large heads or less than attractive neck conformation, look better unbraided if the mane is evenly pulled and trained to fall neatly to one side.

American show hunters and jumpers are braided with many small, flat braids, always on the right side of the neck. The braids should be evenly spaced, be tight, and lie flat against the side of the neck; each braid is about the size of a cigarette and about $1^1/2$ to 2 inches long. The number of braids varies with the size of the horse and the length of his neck, but twenty-five to thirty-five braids is about average. The forelock is almost always braided when the mane is braided, although some jumpers are shown with the forelock free. (A horse with a Roman nose or sloping forehead may look better with the forelock unbraided.) The braids are fastened with yarn, preferably in a color that matches the mane. Brightly colored yarn, rubber bands, tape, or decorations on the mane are as bad as sloppy braiding or long, wild manes—beyond the bounds of good taste!

The tail may be braided, left free, or put up in a mud knot when conditions warrant. A braided tail accentuates the line of the back and the width of the hindquarters; it looks especially nice on a Thoroughbred or Quarter Horse with good hindquarters. Some horses are not flattered by braided tails and may carry them stiffly; these horses are better off with unbraided tails. If the tail is never braided, it may be pulled at the top and sides of the dock in the style popular for dressage horses and eventers. The skirt of the tail may be left in a natural "switch," or it may be "banged off" square across the bottom. Americans usually prefer a longer tail than is seen in some European circles, and they usually square off the tail no higher than the fetlock joint, if they cut it at all.

Mud knots are useful during wet conditions, to prevent the horse from switching mud all over himself and everyone around him. They also flatter a horse with muscular hindquarters.

All braiding must be done neatly to professional standards, or it defeats its purpose. It is better to show with a clean, unbraided mane and tail than to bring a horse out with an incorrect or poorly executed braid job.

Show Grooming Details

Attention to details can make the difference between a first-class appearance and just another entry. Most of these final touches are done by the groom just before the horse enters the show ring.

Coat dressing (usually silicone coat spray, which reflects light and repels dirt) is applied during grooming or after a bath. It is used especially on white markings and on the skirt of the tail. Because silicone makes the hair slippery, it should not be used under the tack.

Before the horse is bridled, the face, muzzle, and ears are cleaned with a damp sponge, and baby oil or highlighter is applied. This makes the fine skin of these areas shiny and accentuates the refinement and expression of the head. The skin beneath the tail is also cleaned and treated with baby oil.

The chestnuts should be cut off level with the skin, and they may be darkened with petroleum jelly or highlighter. Any botfly eggs should be removed during grooming. Any scrapes, cuts, or scars are treated to minimize their appearance.

White markings should be dazzling white. They are shampooed and then treated with silicone coat spray to keep them clean. Cornstarch or French chalk can be sifted into the hair to whiten it; any excess is brushed off the surface.

Quarter marks are sometimes used when the horse is formally turned out (with mane and tail braided). They are applied on the croup using a stencil or a one-inch piece of comb. Quarter marks must be neat, small, and placed high on the croup to call attention to good hindquarter conformation.

The feet are cleaned and freshly painted with a light oil hoof dressing just before entering the ring. (The oil dressing may be omitted when the horse wears bell boots.) Before painting the feet, the groom should check the shoes and studs.

The tack and the rider's boots should be wiped over with leather dressing after the warm-up; care should be taken not to get the reins oily and slippery. A clean sponge and clothes brush can be used to touch up the rider's coat, and a final check is made of his number, his appointments, and the adjustment of the tack.

Tack

Since the rider's control and his safety depend on his tack, he must be aware of the condition and adjustment of every item, even if his groom is responsible for cleaning and caring for the tack. It is good for riders to get into the habit of cleaning their own tack and checking it for condition regularly. Any items showing wear or weakness should be repaired or replaced immediately.

Show tack should be spotlessly clean, soft, supple, and oiled to a deep, mellow color. Metal parts such as bits, buckles, and stirrup irons should be clean and polished. Only good daily care of the tack will produce the supple, comfortable feel and good looks of well-conditioned leather.

Adjustment of tack is just as important as condition. Improperly adjusted equipment irritates the horse and may fail to work as it is intended; it may also slip or give way. Any responsible rider will run his eye over the tack before he mounts, regardless of how briefly he means to ride or whether he has just tacked the horse up himself. Since equipment failure can cause an accident or throw away a class, a rider's check of his tack is just as important as a pilot's preflight inspection of his aircraft. Neither can take time out in midair to attend to something he has overlooked!

Some specific points should be noted in regard to selecting and adjusting tack:

Saddle fit is extremely important to the comfort, performance, and soundness of the horse. It can have a marked effect on the rider's seat and balance, too. The saddle must not press on the horse's withers or spine, no matter how well padded, or it will cause a wither sore; stuffing wither pads under the front of a too wide saddle will not do. The saddle must allow the horse's shoulder blades to rotate freely back when he jumps. A too narrow saddle that jabs the back and shoulder blades can inhibit the horse's use of his front end and cause him to jump and move hollow-backed. While the saddle must be balanced so that the "dip" (the lowest part of the seat) is in the center, too much padding under the cantle can tip it too far forward, jabbing the tree points into the horse's back and throwing the rider too far forward. It is also important that the central channel be wide enough so that the panels do not pinch the horse's spine. No saddle can fit every horse; often bucking, stiffness, or poor movement is the horse's way of expressing discomfort with the rider's favorite saddle.

The saddle pad should fit the saddle with an even one-inch border, and it should be attached to the billets and girth so that it does not bunch up or slip back. White fleece pads are most acceptable. Square "Olympic" style pads are acceptable for jumpers, but they should be plain white with a conservative-colored border. If the horse requires a lift-back pad, foam pad, or back protector, this should be neat and unobtrusive.

The bridle must fit comfortably and allow the bit to work effectively. Snaffle bits should rest high in the mouth, with one or two wrinkles at the corner of the mouth. If the bit is placed lower, the horse may get his tongue over it. If a curb chain is used, all the links must lie flat, and it should be adjusted so that the bit shank rotates forty-five degrees to tighten the curb.

The cavesson should fit snugly enough to prevent the horse from gaping his mouth wide open, but neither a cavesson nor any form of dropped noseband should be cranked so tight that the horse cannot flex and relax his jaw. The chin strap of a flash noseband, dropped noseband, or figure-eight noseband should rest in the chin groove, and the buckle is placed so that it does not lie in the chin groove or irritate the lips. The proper control spot for a dropped noseband is at the point where the nasal bone ends and the cartilage begins; this spot has nerve reflexes which encourage the horse to drop his nose and flex at the poll. If placed lower down, the noseband interferes with the expansion of the nostrils; while it cannot cut off the horse's breathing, it is irritating and may result in head tossing.

The throatlatch should be snug enough to be neat, but it must allow room for the horse to flex at the poll without binding at his throat. The bridle should not pinch or rub at the base of the horse's ears, which may happen if the browband is too short. All strap ends should be confined in keepers and runners, and extra-long ends should be cut off.

When a standing martingale is used, it should only be attached to a cavesson or the cavesson part of a flash noseband—never to a dropped noseband or a figure-eight noseband. (A dropped noseband or figure-eight noseband places the pressure of a standing martingale too low on the nose; also, these nosebands are not designed to withstand the stress a standing martingale puts on them.) The basic adjustment is to fit the martingale so that the strap can be pushed up almost to the horse's throat when his head is in a normal position. (Some horses may need a slightly longer or shorter adjustment.)

A running martingale is normally adjusted so that there is about an inch of play in the martingale when the horse's head is in the normal position and the reins form a straight line from the bit to the rider's elbow. To check the adjustment, pull both martingale rings up to one side; they should just reach to the withers. The martingale should not pull the reins down into a V when the horse's head is in a normal position; a martingale that constantly pulls downward on the reins changes the angle and action of the bit and the rider's contact. For safety's sake, rein stops must be used on the reins to prevent the martingale rings from running up and getting caught on the bit fastenings.

Martingales buckle on the left side, and they should always have a rubber stop at the joining of the neck-strap and chest-strap. This prevents the chest-strap from hanging so low that the horse could catch a foot in it.

Breast collars and hunt breastplates should only be used if they are necessary to keep the saddle from sliding backward—not for decoration. They must be placed carefully to keep them from restricting the free movement of the shoulders when the horse must carry a weight cloth, as the extra weight can make the saddle prone to slip. When an overgirth is used, it must be carefully placed so that it does not interfere with the stirrup bars or slip off the girth. An overgirth requires a girth equipped with keepers through which the overgirth is run.

A jumper that folds his forelegs very tightly may need a chest protector to prevent injuries to his chest, especially when wearing studs. The chest-strap of the martingale or breastplate helps to secure the chest protector in place.

Boots must be secure yet comfortable for the horse. Slip-on (closed) bell boots are the most secure; some other types of fastenings may give way when hit or when they become saturated with mud or water. Bell boots are often used for protection when the horse wears calks or screw-in studs. Tendon boots may be the open-front style, which allows the horse to feel a rub, or the wraparound type. Some horses need the support of bandages instead of or in addition to boots, but these must be expertly applied. Boots should be applied high on the leg and then slipped down into place; they should be checked for tightness after the horse has worked for a few minutes, as the legs may go down as the horse works. Boots must be kept clean and soft on the inside, as mud, sweat, and debris against the skin can cause abrasions and sores.

When one is selecting tack, it is good to remember that plain, classical, workmanlike tack of the best quality will always be in style. The American Jumping Style is not enhanced by garish colors, oddball equipment, or the latest fad.

The Rider:
Attire and Turnout

The American Jumping Style is best exemplified in "workman-like" dress and turnout. Workmanlike means functional, or that which is best for the job, rather than decorative or theatrical. The *American Horse Shows Association Rule Book* states that riders should have "a workmanlike appearance." The rider's attire must be correct, well fitted, and neat and clean.

Boots are a primary item. Plain black dress boots are always correct, and field boots are acceptable; top boots are meant to be worn only with hunt colors or a scarlet coat. Brown, tan, or cordovan boots are permissible for schooling or informal attire, but these colors come and go, while black is always in style.

The fit of the boot is especially important both for looks and for function. The boot must allow the ankle to flex freely, and it should fit the calf closely. It must come as high as possible on the calf without binding at the knee. The ideal fit and look are seldom achieved without custom fitting, modifications to off-the-shelf boots, or great good luck!

Before the rider enters the show ring, his boots should be cleaned off, including the sole of the boot and the stirrup tread. Not only are clean and shiny boots more attractive, but mud and dirt on the sole of the boot can make it easier to lose a stirrup at a critical moment.

Spurs should be worn high on the counter of the boot (just under the horizontal seam), with the spur level (not sloping down or canted up). The spur straps should match the color of the boots and should be snug; extra length should be cut off or tucked neatly under the spur. Loose spurs that slip down encourage a rider to raise his heels and compromise his leg position in order to use his spurs. Slipping spurs also look sloppy.

The breeches should be of a conservative color that is acceptable for the particular class: buff, beige, and gray are best for most purposes. White breeches are only appropriate with a scarlet coat and formal attire or for dressage competitions, and rust is best reserved for informal occasions. The cut of the breeches should be functional and should complement the rider's figure. Stretch fabrics have eliminated the need for wide flares and excessive wrinkles, but a pleated or modified flare breech with an "easy" fit looks better on some figure types than a skintight four-way-stretch type. If the breeches have belt loops, a belt is necessary.

For competition, the rider will wear a riding shirt with a matching choker (for girls and women) or a conservative necktie (for boys and men). The white stock is worn with formal attire and must be neatly tied with the ends anchored beneath the coat. A plain gold stock pin, fastened horizontally, is the only jewelry appropriate for showing.

The riding coat should be of a conservative color: navy, dark gray, dark green, or (for informal classes) tweed. Black is correct for formal occasions, but it is rather severe and may look out of place in informal classes. For Grand Prix, FEI, and other formal jumper classes, only black, dark blue, dark green, or scarlet coats are permitted, and the rider's dress should conform to standards for formal attire (that is, black boots, white breeches, white shirt and stock, and black hunt cap). The fit of the coat is important; it must permit the rider to use his back, shoulders, and arms freely while jumping, but it should be fitted enough to conform neatly to the lines of the back, arms, and body. The sleeves of the jacket must be long enough to cover the rider's arms even when he reaches forward; only a thin line of cuff should show below the sleeve of the jacket.

Gloves should be worn when showing, and many riders will prefer to wear gloves whenever they ride. Gloves should be of a dark, conservative color when worn with a dark coat, as contrast draws attention to the hands and can accentuate any movement. For formal wear, the traditional color is tan. To function well, gloves must fit comfortably without wrinkling or binding, and they should be thin and flexible enough to allow a natural "feel." Nonslip gloves are a necessity when showing in rain or when the reins become slippery with sweat.

The type of stick is a matter of personal preference, but it should be well balanced, easy to hold, and as unobtrusive as possible. Wrist loops are dangerous and should be removed; they can cause a stick to get tangled in the reins in the event of a fall.

A secure, correct, and properly fitted hard hat completes the picture. For show purposes, it should be the black velvet type with a secure harness. Since this item is required by the rules as well as common sense, it makes sense to find a hard hat that protects and fits you well, is as comfortable and attractive as possible, and conforms to current regulations. Then, *wear it—every time you ride!* The primary purpose of a hard hat is to function when things go wrong—to keep an unexpected bump on the head from turning into a major injury. It does no earthly good if the helmet hits the ground before you do, or if it is hanging on the wall in the tack room the one time you really need it.

The entry number must be securely attached so that it is visible to the judges. Back numbers must never be obscured by the rider's hair or attached so that they can fall off or turn over. If the back number does not come equipped with a collar attachment, it should be pinned to the jacket at each corner.

The rider's hair must be neat and fit the general picture. Unless it is quite short, it should be confined in a braid, bun, or hairnet. Even if long hair is worn up under the hat, a hairnet is a good idea—straggling wisps escaping from under the hat or harness do not add to the neat, clean picture, and they are apt to get worse as the day goes on. Any braid, bun, or hairdo should be secured so that it does not bounce and flop around—bouncing braids and bows are inappropriate for anyone past the "short stirrup" age!

Index

George Morris, author of the popular *George Morris Teaches Beginners to Ride* and *Hunter Seat Equitation*, is a former member of the U.S. Equestrian Team. He was a gold medalist in the 1959 Pan American Games, received a silver medal in the 1960 Olympics, and in 1960 won the Grand Prix of Aachen. He now writes frequently for *The Chronicle* and *Practical Horseman* magazine and is an accomplished and successful trainer of jumpers and their riders. He lives in Pittstown, New Jersey.